Li Siyue

Communicating Social Support
in the Digital Age

ZHEJIANG UNIVERSITY PRESS
浙江大学出版社

PREFACE

Supportive communication is a common component of our daily interactions. Every now and then, people would encounter new, challenging, and stressful situations—ranging from having conflict with a relational partner to more significant issues such as battling with a sever health condition. People often cope with these difficult times by seeking support from those in their social networks—their friends, family, and colleagues. Likewise, we often find ourselves responding to others' stress by offering support to them.

Although family and friends have been, and are probably still, a primary source of social support, with the rapid development of the Internet, online supportive communication has become a mass social phenomenon. Going beyond the temporal and spatial constrains, support-seekers can conveniently reach out to a wide range of prospective support-providers online 24 hours and 7 days. Witnessing these important changes in supportive communication, researchers in communication, psychology, public health and other related areas have been delving into this area and making exiting progress.

This book is intended to advance research in the field of online supportive communication by presenting a preliminary theoretical framework which may potentially guide future research in this field. The author has gradually developed a masspersonal model of online supportive communication and conducted a series of empirical research examining different aspects of the model throughout the years. This model, despite in its infancy, takes into account unique characteristics of the Internet in supportive communication. The masspersonal model of online supportive communication will be provided in the opening part of this book. An array of empirical research projects that examine different elements of the framework will be reported in the remainder of the book. For example, two chapters look at how earlier viewers' responses to a support-seeker impact subsequent responses to a support-seeking post. Beyond interaction between support-seekers and support-providers, this book also includes empirical studies that examine the impact of response format (e.g., one-click reaction button vs. textual comment) and context (e.g., Facebook vs. online support forums) on support exchange. As a result, this book represents summative efforts and the latest thinking of the author to advance the field of online supportive communication. It also intends to provide a roadmap for stimulating future research on supportive communication in the digital age.

Table of Contents

Chapter 1   An Overview of Online Supportive Communication

Social support, as an essential form of human communication, plays an important role in people's physical and psychological well-being (MacGeorge, Feng, Burleson, 2011; Rains & Young, 2009; Wright, 2002). As a long-standing topic in communication research, social support has been evolving in a new direction along with the boom of the Internet (Wright & Bell, 2003). Today, the use of online supportive communication has grown into a mass social phenomenon (Barak, Boniel-Nissim, Suler, 2008). Based on a survey conducted by the Pew Internet Research, supportive communication has become a common activity among Internet users.

Support seeking and provision can take place at a distance through a variety of online channels, including but not limited to health blogging (Rains & Keating, 2011, 2015), online support forums (Eichhorn, 2008; Wright & Rains, 2014), social networking sites (High, Oeldorf-Hirsch, Bellur, 2014; Wright et al., 2013), email (Turner et al., 2013), and instant messaging (Feng & Hyun, 2012). Besides the large number of professional health-related support forums (e. g., DailyStrength. org, healthboards. com) through which people try to find support from strangers, other general participatory websites such as Yahoo! Answers (answers. yahoo. com) and Reddit (reddit. com) have become increasingly popular over the years. People seek and provide support on the Internet about almost every possible topic, varying from daily hassles such as having conflicts with romantic partners, to more serious issues such as suffering from a life-threatening disease (Adamic et al. , 2008; Alexander, Peterson, Hollingshead, 2003; Griffiths, Calear, Banfield, 2009). Substantial research evidence has demonstrated the salutary effect of online supportive communication on personal well-being (McMahon et al. , 2005; Rains & Keating, 2011, 2015; Rains & Young, 2009; Wright, 2002).

This chapter conceptualizes online supportive communication and compares the supportive communication that happens on the Internet with that found on other channels. Thereafter, theoretical and pragmatic implications of studying online support are presented, followed by a literature review on online supportive communication. Finally, a masspersonal model of online supportive communication is proposed.

1.1 Defining Online Supportive Communication

Online supportive communication has drawn a great amount of research attention (Barak, Boniel-Nissim, Suler, 2008; Rains & Young, 2009; Walther & Boyd, 2002; Wright & Bell, 2003). However, a well-established definition of online supportive communication has not emerged. Supportive communication in general has been defined as "verbal and nonverbal behavior produced with the intention of providing assistance to others perceived as needing that aid" (Burleson & MacGeorge, 2002). This broad definition applies to supportive communication that occurs in any form (e. g. , face-to-face, telephone, and online). Online supportive communication is a subcategory of supportive communication which takes place through a specific medium—the Internet. It can thus be defined as a process through which people produce any verbal and nonverbal behavior *online* with an intention to seek help from others or provide assistance for others in need of support.

Three implications flow from this definition. First, it highlights the importance of communicative outcomes (i. e. , verbal and nonverbal behaviors) rather than perceptual outcomes. Social support literature from a psychological perspective tends to emphasize the impact of cognitive and emotional factors on personal health (Brock & Lawrence, 2010; MacGeorge, Feng, Burleson, 2011). In contrast, a communication perspective primarily focuses on a "relatively direct connection between communication and well-being" (MacGeorge, Feng, Burleson, 2011).

Second, online supportive communication is characterized by people's intentional acts to seek or provide assistance (MacGeorge, Feng, Burleson, 2011). This feature emphasizes the role of intentionality from either a support-seeker or a provider. Any intentional behavior of support seeking, regardless of being received or not by others, is considered as a supportive communication behavior. Meanwhile, a helper's intentional response to a support-seeker is part of supportive communication.

Third, and probably the most unique feature of this conceptualization resides in its focus on a single medium. Supportive communication on the Internet may take a variety of forms (Bo, 2008), such as online support forums (Campbell & Wright, 2002; Chung, 2013), health blogging (Rains, 2013; Rains & Keating, 2015), and instant messaging (Feng & Hyun, 2012). This definition, however, only includes supportive communication that remains online. Supportive interactions which occur across media involving the Internet (e. g., switching from face-to-face to the Internet) are beyond the scope of this definition.

1.2 Advantages of Online Supportive Communication

Online supportive communication, like its counterparts in other forms, can take place in both weak-tie (Rains & Keating, 2011; Robinson et al., 2011; Wright, Rains, Banas, 2010; Wright & Rains, 2014) and strong-tie relationships (Feng & Hyun, 2012; Rains & Keating, 2011; Wright et al., 2013). However, the Internet possesses unique features that can facilitate effective supportive exchange.

Compared to other channels, the Internet provides people with relatively easy access to support exchange (Barak, Boniel-Nissim, Suler, 2008; Mikal et al., 2013; Rains & Young, 2009; Walther & Boyd, 2002). Many forms of online support (e. g., email, online support forum, and blogging) are carried out in an asynchronous manner, allowing people to have access to these platforms 24 hours, 7 days a week, and at times most convenient to them (Turner, Grube, Meyers, 2001; White & Dorman, 2001). Interactants are free to leave and reenter an interaction anytime and are not under pressure of immediate responses (Barak, Boniel-Nissim, Suler, 2008; Walther & Boyd, 2002). Having plenty of time to compose a message may have the therapeutic value (Barak, Boniel-Nissim, Suler, 2008; Wright & Bell, 2003) because "the energy and time a person takes in the very act of formulating and expressing his or her distress may provide at least some release from tension and anxiety" (Binik et al., 1997). On support forums, the asynchronous feature can allow multiple people to respond to the same message, which increases the number of potential helpers (Wright & Bell, 2003). Besides the minimal temporal constraints, online support is free from geographic impositions (Turner et al., 2001; White & Dorman, 2001). People with mobility problems or caregiving responsibilities can equally participate at a distance without travel.

The distinction of the Internet is also manifested in its high level of anonymity (Barak, Boniel-Nissim, Suler, 2008; Tanis, 2008). Because most contextual and nonverbal cues are filtered out in text based on computer-mediated communication (Walther & Parks, 2002), people do not necessarily know one another's offline identities (Barak, Boniel-Nissim, Suler, 2008). Especially when interacting with weak ties, people are not obliged to reveal their personal information unless they are willing to do so (Tanis, 2008). A sense of anonymity makes people feel more comfortable sharing embarrassing or stigmatized information, contributing to increased intimacy and honesty in self-disclosure (Rains & Young, 2009;

Walther & Boyd, 2002).

A more compelling feature is the Internet's capacity of providing people with a substantially extended and diverse network of potential support sources, creating more opportunities for support-seekers to receive needed help (Turner et al., 2001). This advantage is more salient when people participate in online support groups. Unlike traditional face-to-face support groups which can only accommodate a few people (usually no more than 10 or 11 individuals), online support forums enable a support-seeker to reach out to a large number of potential helpers (Turner et al., 2001; White & Dorman, 2001), brought together by similar experiences and stressors on a certain topic (Walther & Boyd, 2002). Common interests among these users thereby increase the possibility for individuals to find a match with their specific type of concerns (Turner et al., 2001).

1.3 Theoretical and Pragmatic Implications

Online supportive communication is a theoretically and pragmatically important topic to study. Supportive communication is a fundamental form of human interaction from which we can explore and understand the basic communication processes such as message production and reception (Burleson, Albrecht, Sarason, 1994; MacGeorge, Feng, Burleson, 2011). Research on online supportive communication has studied the communication process from different aspects, including support seeking (Rains & Keating, 2015; Tanis, 2008), support provision (Eichhorn, 2008), supportive message processing (Spottswood et al., 2013), and the interaction between support-seekers and support-providers (Feng, Li, Li, 2016; Tichon & Shapiro, 2003). However, extant literature largely focuses on antecedents (e. g., personality traits) or outcomes (e. g., mental and physical health) of online support rather than the supportive communication process (Feng, Li, Li, 2016). More research should be devoted to the basic communication process in online supportive communication, such as interactions between support-seekers and support-providers or among support-providers themselves.

As an interdisciplinary area, online supportive communication integrates interpersonal communication, mediated communication, and health communication. The interdisciplinary feature makes online support a relatively unique area to study and have the potential to integrate theories from different areas and generate its own. So far, most studies on supportive communication "have been descriptive in nature, and they have not linked findings to a broader theoretical framework, despite a vast number of theories in both the areas of social support and computer-mediated communication" (Wright & Bell, 2003). Therefore, more research needs to be devoted to theorizing online supportive communication. For example, the idea of "masspersonal" communication can be extended to capture unique features of online supportive communication. That is, online support forum provides an interpersonal channel because it enables people to communicate supports at an interpersonal level. Meanwhile, other users can observe the interpersonal interaction because of the publicity of the messages on forums. To go beyond being descriptive, more research is needed to theorize online supportive communication.

Online supportive communication is also a pragmatically important phenomenon to study. The movement of online support has become a mass social phenomenon with a rapid growth of people exchanging social support online (Barak, Boniel-Nissim, Suler, 2008). National Cancer Institute indicated that 7.5 million American adults sought peer support about a health issue during 2012. Substantial research has suggested that online supportive communication facilitates personal health and well-being (McMahon et al., 2005; Rains & Keating, 2011, 2015; Rains & Young, 2009; Wright, 2002). Online support exchange benefits both physical and psychological health, including increased social support, reduced negative mood, enhanced quality of life, and higher self-efficacy in coping (Carlbring et al., 2005; McMahon et al., 2005; Rains & Young, 2009; Shaw et al., 2006; Wright, 2002). In order to maximize the positive impact of online supportive communication on personal health, we need to better understand this communication phenomenon.

Despite gaining increasing popularity, online supportive communication is not without limitations (Coulson & Knibb, 2007; Lewandowski et al., 2011; Wright, 2002; Wright & Bell, 2003). Due to a vast array of available information (Metzger & Flanagin, 2011) yet fewer nonverbal cues presented online (Wright & Bell, 2003), the issue of information credibility is more prominent in the virtual world. People need to make evaluations on accuracy of information as well as validity of experiences and feelings shared by remote others online (Wright & Bell, 2003). Given that perceived credibility significantly influences a support-seeker's perception of received support (Campbell & Wright, 2002; Wang et al., 2008), it is important to provide people with practical guidance on making better judgments on online support messages. The other issue on online support pertains to the presence of hostile messages (Aakhus & Rumsey, 2010; Wright & Bell, 2003). A lack of nonverbal cues in textual computer-mediated communication may lead to a dehumanization perception of the unseen interactant and create the feeling of minimal relational obligations (Mesch & Beker, 2010; Wright & Bell, 2003), which in turn increases hostile communication on support forums (Lewandowski et al., 2011). Understanding the mechanisms of online supportive communication may help shape a constructive environment for support exchange as well as reduce the occurrence of hostile communication online (Aakhus & Rumsey, 2010).

1.4 Extant Literature on Online Supportive Communication

The literature on online support has grown tremendously over the last decade. Extant literature has focused largely on three general issues. The first issue pertains to the characteristics of online support-seekers and their motivations to engage in online support (Buchanan & Coulson, 2007;

Chung, 2013; Coulson & Knibb, 2007; Wright, 2002). Demographic characteristics such as age and gender are associated with usage of online support. Empirical research has suggested a negative association between age and preference for weak-tie support online (Wright et al., 2010). In particular, younger people are more inclined to seek support from online weak-ties. Conducting social network analysis, Durant, McCray and Safran (2012) revealed that men preferred larger and less intimate interactions on support forums whereas women in general opted for fewer and more intimate connection on these platforms. Research has also suggested the impact of individual differences on usage of online support. For example, when in need of mental health support, those who have more social stigma concerns are more likely to use online support forums than those who have less social stigma concerns (DeAndrea, 2015). In addition, those who are not facing a terminal disease are more likely to seek weak-tie support online (Wright et al., 2010). People who are unsatisfied with support received in offline relationships have a stronger preference for online support (Chung, 2013). Besides users' characteristics, substantial research has revealed a number of motives for people to engage in online social support, among which exchanging information and sharing emotion are the most common motives (Buchanan & Coulson, 2007; Chung, 2013).

The second line of research has primarily focused on physical and psychological outcomes attributed to online supportive communication, yielding substantial amount of evidence indicating that online support, much like its face-to-face counterpart, can have a positive impact on individuals' physical and psychological well-being (Rains & Keating, 2011; Rains & Young, 2009; Wright, 2002). For example, based on a meta-analysis of 28 studies, Rains and Young (2009) concluded that participation in online support groups contributed to increased social support and self-efficacy to manage one's health condition as well as decreased depression. Likewise, emotional support in emails from health providers are associated with improved health of diabetes patients (Turner et al., 2013). Health bloggers who lack strong-tie support offline report a lower level of loneliness and a higher degree of personal growth when they receive more support from blog readers (Rains & Keating, 2011). Internet users who have more social interactions on social networking sites (e. g. , Facebook) tend to have more positive affect and thereby increased life satisfaction (Oh, Ozkaya, LaRose, 2014).

The third issue concerns features of online support messages. For example, many studies have tried to identify different types of support, as well as the relative predominance of each type of support (Bunde et al. , 2007; Donovan et al. , 2014). In general, informational and emotional support are the most prevalent in health-related contexts online, with some variations depending on the nature of illness (Rains, Peterson, Wright, 2015). For example, emotional support is more common among people facing terminal illness; whereas informational support is more frequent among people with chronic conditions (Rains, Peterson, Wright, 2015). It is worth noting that support messages typically contain more than one type of support, with a combination of informational, emotional, esteem support being the most common form (Donovan et al. , 2014). Moving beyond typologies of online social support, some researchers examined the language style matching (e. g. , articles, propositions, pronouns) between health bloggers and their readers in their posts as a predictor of bloggers' perceived support (Rains, Peterson, Wright, 2015).

1.5 Limitation of Extant Literature

While the extant literature has offered valuable insights on the subject of online supportive communication, at least three major limitations merit scholarly attention. One notable limitation with prior research on online support is that it has focused primarily on precedents (e. g. , personality traits and motivations) (Wright, 2002; Wright et al. , 2010) and outcomes of online supportive communication (Womble et al. , 2004). Scant research attention has been given to understanding the online supportive communication process (Feng, Li, Li, 2016). In particular, very little is known about how the various features and aspects of online support-seeking (e. g. , anonymity, asynchronicity, user-generated comments) can affect online support provision, how support-seekers interact with support-providers, and how support providers interact among themselves. One such known study investigated how support-seekers' profile features could influence viewers' perceptions of the support-seeker and thereby the quality of support messages that they provide (Feng, Li, Li, 2016). Feng, Li and Li's (2016) study found that support-seeking posts accompanied with a user profile containing more personal identity cues (user ID containing first name and portrait picture) tended to elicit support with higher levels of person-centeredness and politeness than support-seeking posts whose user profiles contain fewer personal identity cues. In this book, the author aimed to investigate how unique features of online "masspersonal communication," such as user-generated responses and support-seekers' reply to those responses, may influence online support provision, and explore the psychological mechanisms that underlie the impact.

The second limitation is that, in terms of methodology, the majority of past studies have relied heavily on the use of surveys or content analysis to study online support (Tanis, 2008; Tichon & Shapiro, 2003; Wright, 2000). As a result, it is difficult to assess causality among different factors or to identify the mechanisms underlying online supportive communication. Apart from previous research, research reported in this book primarily employed experimental designs. This methodology allows researchers to (a) examine online supportive communication in a much more ecologically appropriate manner; (b) manipulate central variables of interest (e. g. , others' comments and support-seekers' reply) while at the same time controlling factors that are not the focus of examination in this study but can potentially influence online support provision (e. g. , content of support-seeking posts, profile features of support-seekers); and (c) empirically assess the potential causal link between antecedents and outcome variables relating to online support.

Third, relatively little research has been done to understand specific features of online support messages beyond their typological categorization, with some exceptions of Rains' (2013) and Feng, Li, and Li's (2016) recent works. In particular, few studies have examined how support-seeking and provision messages are qualitatively different. This book attempts to address this limitation by developing a more comprehensive assessment of the features of support messages than that used in past research. The quality of a support message has conventionally been differentiated by person-centeredness (Burleson, 1982). Researchers who study supportive communication have traditionally operationalized this concept by assessing the extent to which a support message explicitly acknowledges the target's feelings and helps the target reappraise the distressing situation (for a review, see MacGeorge, Feng, Burleson, 2011). Burleson (1982) developed a nine-level hierarchy to assess the extent of person-centeredness in support messages. Although the person-centeredness hierarchy (Burleson, 1982) has been shown to be a very useful tool for capturing variation in quality of emotion-focused verbal support messages, it did not provide an assessment of message variation in action-focused verbal support messages. Besides seeking comfort, support-seekers often look for support on actions (Eichhorn, 2008; Ginossar, 2008). For instance, a support-seeker who wants to switch job may seek validation of this intended behavior from others. The extent to which a support-provider legitimizes or supports the target's enacted and/or intended behavior manifests another important dimension of message supportiveness. In addition, although substantial research has demonstrated the crucial role of politeness in supportive interactions, especially in the context of advice-giving and -receiving (for a review, see MacGeorge, Feng, Thompson, 2008), it is only until very recently that exhibition of politeness was identified and assessed as a dimension of support message distinct from the emotion-focused verbal person-centeredness (Feng,

Li, Li, 2016). Given these considerations, the current work proposes a multi-dimensional typology to assess person-centeredness of support messages.

1.6 Theoretical Frameworks on Online Supportive Communication

The phenomenon of online support has earned substantial interests from researchers (Barak, Boniel-Nissim, Suler, 2008; Rains & Young, 2009; Walther & Boyd, 2002; Wright & Bell, 2003). However, most studies on supportive communication "have been descriptive in nature, and they have not linked findings to a broader theoretical framework, despite a vast number of theories in both the areas of social support and computer-mediated communication" (Wright & Bell, 2003). Only a handful of studies have attempted to incorporate theoretical frameworks in explaining and predicting results on online support (Eichhorn, 2008; Turner et al. , 2001; Wang et al. , 2008). The following section reviews major theories that have been applied to the field of online support.

1. 6. 1 Hyperpersonal Model

The hyperpersonal model (Walther, 1996), as an influential framework in computer-mediated communication, has been applied to explain the phenomenon of online support (Eichhorn, 2008; Turner et al. , 2001; VanLear, et al. , 2005; Walther & Boyd, 2002; Wang et al. , 2008). The hyperpersonal model (Walther, 1996) argues that people can develop more intimate relationships online than face-to-face. Four characteristics are proposed in this model to account for hyperpersonal communication: (a) senders engaging in selective self-presentation due to the lack of nonverbal cues, (b) receivers overattributing the similarity and liking of senders, (c) asynchronous medium enabling interactants to communicate at their own time, and (d) a feedback loop intensifying established impression and intimacy.

When applied to online supportive communication (Turner et al., 2001; VanLear et al., 2005; Wang et al., 2008), the hyperpersonal model receives some empirical support as people sometimes report having a closer relationship with online support network relative than offline counterparts (Turner et al., 2001; Wright, 2000).

The hyperpersonal model provides a potential framework to explain why support-seekers can develop a close relationship with online support-providers, especially with those unbeknownst to each other offline (Wright & Bell, 2003). Specifically, this model relates the unique features of online channels to the development of online supportive relationship. The absence of abundant personal identity cues online makes people focus more on shared similarities with others (e. g., similar experience or stressor) and exaggerate these similarities to create a more intimate relationship. In addition, the affordance of asynchronicity allows careful craft and edit of messages to better express personal thoughts and feelings (Walther, Boyd, 2002).

The hyperpersonal model has mostly been applied to ongoing relationships (Walther & Boyd, 2002). That is, as people have continuous interactions online, the hyperpersonal effect is more likely to manifest (Walther, 1997). Many forms of online supportive communication, represented by open support forums (e. g., Yahoo! Answer), predominantly involve one-shot interaction among strangers and do not provide plenty time for them to know one another during the process of supportive communication. Under these circumstances, the hyperpersonal model is of relatively low utility to explain the short-term interaction among unknown support-seekers and -providers.

1. 6. 2 Social Presence

Social presence, an influential construct in media studies, has also been employed as a theoretical framework for research on online support

(Feng, Li, Li, 2016). Originated from the social presence theory (Short, Williams, Christie, 1976), social presence is defined as "the degree of salience of the other person in the interaction and the consequent salience of the interpersonal relationships" and operationalized in terms of how "sociable, warm, sensitive, and personal" people perceive the communication medium to be. While the original theory emphasizes social presence as a feature attached to a medium (Short, William, Christic, 1976; Walther, 1992), more recent work tends to define social presence as the psychological distance between an individual and his or her interactional counterpart, and stresses the sense of copresence within a given communication situation (Lee & Jang, 2013; Lee & Nass, 2005). Feng, Li and Li (2016) postulated that perceived social presence of an online support seeker may influence the quality of provided-social support. Their findings suggest that support-seekers who contain more personal identity cues (e. g. , a portrait picture and a first name ID) in their user profiles elicit higher perceived social presence from viewers, which in turn, leads to higher person-centered and more polite supportive messages than support-seekers who do not include these cues in their profiles.

Social presence is a useful construct to examine online users' perceptions of their communication partners, which functions as a bridge to connect the various characteristics of online support channels (e. g. , the lack of cues) and actual production of supportive messages. In other words, we can have a better understanding of the underlying mechanism through which different features of online support channels influence the process of online support exchange (Feng, Li, Li, 2016). However, social presence as a single construct may be inadequate to guide research on online supportive communication as a whole. Social presence itself only concerns the perception of a relational partner (Lee & Jang, 2013; Lee & Nass, 2005). To explain the process of supportive communication in a more systematic way, researchers need to develop a more comprehensive theory on social presence, with a consideration of both the antecedents and communication outcomes of social presence in online support.

1. 6. 3 Optimal Matching Theory

Online supportive communication, as an intersection of both computer-mediated communication and social support, also attempts to integrate traditional social support theories into its literature (Eichhorn, 2008; Turner et al., 2001). Optimal matching theory (Cutrona & Russell, 1990) posits that certain types of social support are most effective when matched with certain types of stressors. This theory suggests that three characteristics of stressors, including desirability (i. e., extent to which negative emotions are engendered), controllability (i. e., extent to which an individual has controlled over the outcome), and domain (i. e., whether the stressor is related to assets, relationships, achievement, or social roles), determine the types of support needed for positive health outcomes. Among the three characteristics, controllability exerts the most significant influence on determining needed support type. People with controllable stressors desire more instrumental and informational support whereas people with uncontrollable stressors demand more emotional support (Cutrona & Russell, 1990). When applied to online support, this theory gains some support (Eichhorn, 2008; Turner et al., 2001). Because eating disorder is a controllable stressor, Eichhorn (2008) hypothesized that people on the discussion boards of eating disorder would provide more informational support than other types of support, a prediction validated in the study. Turner and his associates (2001) employed optimal matching model in a broader sense to study support provided online versus offline. Instead of focusing on specific types of support, their study explored whether people who would engage in more online support seeking when face-to-face support could not meet their needs. They found that people would read more on support listserv when they had low-quality support from face-to-face partners. This result implies that people may find a certain match of needed help online that is missing in face-to-face support.

Optimal matching theory is useful as it can in part explain people's motivation to seek social support online. Online support sometimes can serve as an effective supplement to insufficient face-to-face support (Rains & Keating, 2011; Turner et al., 2001). In addition, it points out a possible direction on how to provide effective support online: matching support type with needed support (Cutrona & Russell, 1990).

Despite its appeal in the literature, this theory provides limited guidance on research regarding online supportive communication. First, this theory oversimplifies the nature of stressors and supports (MacGeorge, Feng, Burleson, 2011). Both stressors and supportive messages are complex to the extent that they may involve different types or dimensions (Feng, 2009). For instance, a patient with diabetes may suffer from both physical and mental stress and thus need informational as well as emotional support. An arbitrary categorization of stressors or supportive messages into only one category (Eichhorn, 2008) may not accurately reflect the reality of supportive communication.

Second, the matching model emphasizes a matching on support type whereas ignores the quality of supportive messages. According to the communication perspective on supportive communication, supportive messages differ substantially in terms of quality, leading to distinct impacts on support effectiveness (MacGeorge, Feng, Burleson, 2011). Optimal matching theory is mute on this matter and thus inadequate to account for the features of supportive communication.

Still problematic is its weak connection to online support. As a general theory on social support, optimal matching model does not take into account distinctive features of online support channels that may contribute to the uniqueness of online support exchange. In other words, this theory fails to differentiate supportive communication in cyberspace from other media and thus undermines the importance of online supportive communication as an independent research area.

1. 6. 4 Dual Process Models

To explain online supportive message processing, researchers also introduce persuasion theories into this area. The Internet fosters support exchange among weak-ties (Wright & Bell, 2003), who can provide a variety of relevant information and experience. Nevertheless, receivers may have concerns over the credibility of supportive messages (Metzger & Flanagin, 2011; Wright & Bell, 2003). Dual process models, including the elaboration likelihood model (Petty & Cacioppo, 1986) and the dual process model of social support (Bodie & Burleson, 2008), have been applied to explain how people make judgments of online supportive messages. According to these models, people utilize two distinctive routes when exposed to a message, the central route and the peripheral route. The central route is taken when the individual forms an opinion based on a consideration of the information related to the issue, including arguments and evidence presented in the message (e. g. , feasibility of advice). When the person is unable or unwilling to process the message in this way, a decision may be formulated on the basis of peripheral cues (e. g. , expertise, user-generated star ratings, and so forth). Jang and Walther (2012) studied how people processed advice on Yahoo! Answers within the framework of dual process models yet did not find much empirical support for the models.

Given that dual process models take into account the complexity of online support information such as user-generated comments and star-ratings, these models have the potential to orient research on message processing in online supportive communication. Researchers can use these models to study how people evaluate and make choice of different types of support information (especially those with contradictory information).

However, three limitations of these models in relation to online support cannot be ignored. First, the distinction between central and peripheral cues is blurred (Petty & Wegener, 1999). For instance, the conventionally regarded peripheral cues such as source credibility can also serve as a central argument if this piece of information is given extensive thoughts. Some researchers in their study discovered a stronger impact of star-ratings on perceptions of advice utility among individuals with high issue-involvement relative to individuals with low issue-involvement. They speculated that star-ratings may not operationalize as traditional peripheral cues, but rather function as central cues. The ambiguity in term of differentiating central from peripheral cues online makes it difficult to predict how people process supportive information online.

Second, the limitation pertains to the motivation in message processing. People may have relatively low motivation to process a message when the issue is of low relevance (Petty & Cacioppo, 1986). However, when people actively seek social support online, the issue relevance is expected to be relatively high. Due to the lack of nonverbal cues in online textual communication, people often need to explicitly seek support online to increase the opportunity of receiving assistance. These active support-seekers are thus expected to have a high motivation to process supportive messages. Seen in this light, the variations in motivation to process online supportive messages may be small, causing a less utility of the motivation variable in studying this phenomenon.

Third, the variations in ability to process online supportive messages may decrease as well. An individual's ability to process information centrally is dependent on distractions and his prior knowledge (Petty & Cacioppo, 1986). The asynchronous feature of most online communication forms enables audience to control their interaction time (Walther, 1996). A highly motivated support-seeker can process the recordable messages when he is best able to control distractions. In addition, a highly motivated support-seeker can search additional information through different venues to facilitate his understanding of supportive messages. Given these considerations, most support-seekers online should be able to process supportive messages centrally, especially in an asynchronous mode.

To date, research on online supportive communication has been making slow progress in theorizing this phenomenon. Most extant theories applied to online support contain certain merits and limitations (Eichhorn, 2008; Turner et al., 2001). This field demands a more compelling theory that can account for the unique features of online communication as well as supportive communication (Wright & Bell, 2003).

1.7 A Masspersonal Model of Online Supportive Communication

A masspersonal model of online supportive communication is proposed in this book for the first time to account for the evolving dynamics of online support exchange. While face-to-face support exchange typically involves one-on-one or one-to-several communication, support seeking and provision online may engage a much broader audience who can potentially provide support. For instance, a distressed individual may post an upsetting status on social media such as Facebook or WeChat Moments which can be accessible to a wide audience. In addition, those who post support-seeking messages on online support forums may have access to an even larger audience among whom many are unknown to the support-seeker. In other words, the typical interpersonal communication exhibited in face-to-face support exchange may have been supplemented by features of mass communication (e. g., broadcasting messages to a wide audience) in an online environment. At the same time, online supportive communication is not entirely mass communication because audience who view a support-seeking message may choose to engage in public or private interaction with the support-seeker. Even if a support-provider leaves a comment to the support-seeking message in a public way, the comment itself may only be intended to target the support-seeker and thus exhibits features of interpersonal communication.

Given the convergence of interpersonal communication and mass communication in the context of online support, a model of masspersonal communication in online support is proposed here. The concept of masspersonal communication was first introduced to capture the unique phenomenon of online communication by bridging mass-interpersonal divide. This concept highlights the intersection between mass communication and interpersonal communication. The model of masspersonal communication (O'Sullivan & Carr, 2018) challenges the assumption that whether or not individuals engage in mass or interpersonal communication is determined by the nature of communication channels. That is, the conventional mass channels can be used for interpersonal communication and the conventional interpersonal channels can be used for mass communication. For instance, radio as a broadcasting channel can entail interpersonal communication between an anchor and an individual audience. Emails intended for one target can be forwarded to a large audience.

According to the model of masspersonal communication, communication differs on two dimensions—perceived exclusivity of message access and message personalization (O'Sullivan & Carr, 2018). Perceived exclusivity of message access concerns the extent to which a message is accessible by others at any particular time. This dimension varies between being exclusively accessible to an individual to the broadest range of being accessible to everyone and anyone. Message personalization is conceptualized as the extent to which a message is tailored to meet specific needs of a particular individual. A highly personalized message reflects the uniqueness of a receiver whereas a low-personalized message is not tailored for any particular receivers. Based on the variations in these two dimensions, O'Sullivan and Carr (2018) divided communication into three quadrants: mass communication (i. e. , low perceived exclusivity of message access, low message personalization), interpersonal communication (i. e. , high perceived exclusivity of message access, high message personalization), and masspersonal communication (i. e. , low perceived exclusivity of message access, high message personalization).

The idea of masspersonal communication takes into account unique features of online communication and is borrowed into the current work regarding online supportive communication. First, online supportive communication, especially those carried out in public and semipublic forms, is characterized by low perceived exclusivity of message access. For instance, a distressed person may send out a support-seeking message on Facebook Timeline or WeChat Moments where a broad audience can view the message. In addition, when a helper responds to a support-seeking message, the response is also visible to others who are in the same circle. The low perceived exclusivity of message access may have altered the ways that people seek and provide social support in online platforms. From the perspective of support-seekers, a broad access to a support-seeking message from others may motivate a support-seeker to care more about their self-presentations. They may strategically consider how to balance their needs of support-elicitation and concerns over positive self-presentation when composing messages (Oh, Ozkaya, LaRose, 2014). From the perspective of support-providers, the visibility of others' feedback may influence their perceptions of a support-seeker and their subsequent responses to the target (Li & Feng, 2015).

High message personalization, as the second characteristic of masspersonal communication, also permeates online supportive communication. Communication involves takes and turns. Online viewers may choose to respond to a support-seeking message with highly personalized content that directly addresses the support-seeker's concerns and needs. In addition, support-seekers may also choose to respond to others' replies with highly personalized messages, such as directly answering a support-provider's question or providing further information upon a support-provider's request. The extent to which messages are personalized to specific targets has the potential to influence the quality of support provision.

Figure 1. 1 is presented to further illustrate the main ideas in the masspersonal model of online supportive communication. The figure in the in the left circle represents a support-seeker who initiates the online supportive communication. When a support-seeker submits the original post online, the post becomes a piece of mass communication message because the post is viewable to a potentially large audience, which in this diagram is represented by the right circle, and which is comprised of anyone who has access to the post. They represent the potential support-providers. It is possible that a support-seeking post will target one or more individuals in the audience. The dotted lines from the support-seeker to the specific individuals in the audience illustrate this possibility. The dotted lines represent potential responses from support-providers to the support-seeker. These lines are crossed because support-providers' responses might influence each other. The dotted lines within the right circle represent interactions that may occur among potential support-providers. Double arrows are used to illustrate the idea that the role of support-seekers and support-providers is interchangeable. A support-provider may take the role of a support-seeker at a certain point, and vice versa. The model also suggests that various characteristics of a support-seeker, such as their past experiences, culture, attitudes, and values should affect their message production and reception. Likewise, the support-providers' characteristics and attributes may also affect their support provision. Context on the top right includes not only virtual settings such as the different types of online platforms; it also contains relational context such as the past history of interaction among the communicators, as well as cultural context such as community norms governing the forum users' interactions. Noise refers to any possible interruption of effective communication, such as the mood of a communicator (e. g. , people in a sad mood may less likely to provide support) or technological barriers during communication.

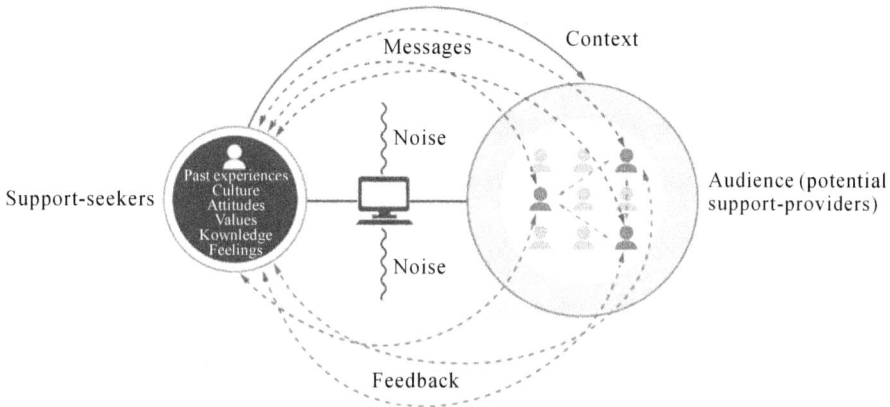

Figure 1.1   A masspersonal model of online supportive communication

The descriptions aforementioned present some preliminary efforts to synthesize key factors regarding online supportive communication into a comprehensive framework. Compared with other theories applied to the field of online support, this model highlights the unique features of online communication in supportive communication. Specifically, the convergence of mass and interpersonal communication may reshape the dynamics of online support exchange and bring new opportunities to support-seekers. Further, the proposed model acknowledges both roles of sender and receiver in online supportive communication. Interactions between support-seekers and support-providers, as well as among prospective support-providers can mutually influence perceptions of support-seekers and support provision. The masspersonal model of online supportive communication, as a newly proposed framework, awaits more work for validation and modification. This book reports a series of empirical research which provides some initial efforts to examine the key elements in this model and strives to provide a more comprehensive understanding on the phenomenon of online support exchange.

23

References

Aakhus, M., and Rumsey, E. (2010). Crafting supportive communication online: A communication design analysis of conflict in an online support group. *Journal of Applied Communication Research*, 38, 65-84. doi: 10.1080/00909880903483581.

Adamic, L. A., Zhang, J., Bakshy, E., and Ackerman, M. S. (2008). Knowledge sharing and Yahoo Answers: Everyone knows something. In: *Proceedings of the International World Wide Web Conference*. Beijing: ACM, pp. 665-674.

Alexander, S. C., Peterson, J. L., and Hollingshead, A. B. (2003). Help is at your keyboard: Support groups on the Internet. In: L. R. Frey, ed., *Group Communication in Context: Studies of Bona Fide Groups*. Mahwah, NJ: Erlbaum, pp. 309-334.

Barak, A., Boniel-Nissim, M., and Suler, J. (2008). Fostering empowerment in online support groups. *Computers in Human Behavior*, 24, 1867-1883. doi: http://dx.doi.org/10.1016/j.chb.2008.02.004.

Bo, X. (2008). Multimodal computer-mediated communication and social support among older Chinese Internet users. *Journal of Computer-Mediated Communication*, 13, 728-750. doi: 10.1111/j.1083-6101.2008.00417.x.

Bodie, G. D., and Burleson, B. R. (2008). Explaining variations in the effects of supportive messages: A dual-process framework. In: C. Beck, ed., *Communication Yearbook* 32. New York: Routledge, pp. 354-398.

Binik, Y. M., Cantor, J., Ochs, E., and Meana, M. (1997). From the couch to the keyboard: Psychotherapy in cyberspace. In: S. Kiesler, ed., *Culture of the Internet*. Mahwah, NJ: Lawrence Erlbaum, pp. 71-100.

Brock, R. L., and Lawrence, E. (2010). Support adequacy in marriage:

Observing the platinum rule. In K. T. Sullivan, and J. Davila, eds.,
Support Processes in Intimate Relationships. New York: Oxford University
Press, pp. 3-25.

Buchanan, H., and Coulson, N. S. (2007). Accessing dental anxiety
online support groups: An exploratory qualitative study of motives and
experiences. *Patient Education and Counseling*, 66(3), 263-269. doi:
10.1016/j.pec.2006.12.011.

Bunde, M., Suls, J., Martin, R., and Barnett, K. (2007). Online hysterectomy
support: Characteristics of website experiences. *Cyberpsychology & Behavior*,
10(1), 80-85. doi: 10.1089/cpb.2006.9989.

Burleson, B. R. (1982). The development of comforting communication
skills in childhood and adolescence. *Child Development*, 53, 1578-
1588. doi: 10.1111/1467-8624.ep8588469.

Burleson, B. R., Albrecht, T. L., and Sarason, I. G. (1994). *Communication
of Social Support: Messages, Interactions, Relationships, and Community*.
Thousand Oaks, CA: Sage.

Burleson, B. R., and MacGeorge, E. L. (2002). Supportive communication.
In: M. L. Knapp, and J. A. Daly, eds., *Handbook of Interpersonal
Communication*. 3rd ed. Thousand Oaks, CA: Sage, pp. 374-424.

Campbell, K., and Wright, K. B. (2002). On-line support groups: An
investigation of relationships among source credibility, dimensions of
relational communication, and perceptions of emotional support.
Communication Research Reports, 19, 183-193. doi: 10.1080/08824
090209384846.

Carlbring, P., Nilsson-Ihrfelt, E., Waara, J., Kollenstam, C., Buhrman,
M., Kaldo, V., and Andersson, G. (2005). Treatment of panic disorder:
Live therapy vs. self-help via the Internet. *Behaviour Research and Therapy*,
43, 1321-1333. doi: 10.1016/j.brat.2004.10.002.

Chung, J. E. (2013). Social interaction in online support groups: Preference
for online social interaction over offline social interaction. *Computers in
Human Behavior*, 29, 1408-1414. doi: 10.1016/j.chb.2013.01.019.

Coulson, N. S., and Knibb, R. C. (2007). Coping with food allergy: Exploring the role of the online support group. *Cyberpsychology & Behavior*, 10, pp.145-148.

Cutrona, C., and Russell, D. (1990). Type of social support and specific stress: Towards a theory of optimal matching. In: B. Sarason, I. Sarason, and G. Pierce, eds., *Social Support: An Interactional View*. New York: Wiley, pp. 319-366.

DeAndrea, D. C. (2015). Testing the proclaimed affordances of online support groups in a nationally representative sample of adults seeking mental health assistance. *Journal of Health Communication*, 20(2), 147-156. doi: 10.1080/10810730.2014.914606.

Donovan, E. E., LeFebvre, L., Tardif, S., Brown, L. E., and Love, B. (2014). Patterns of social support communicated in response to expressions of uncertainty in an online community of young adults with cancer. *Journal of Applied Communication Research*, 42(4), 432-455. doi: 10.1080/00909882.2014.929725.

Durant, K. T., McCray, A. T., and Safran, C. (2012). Identifying gender-preferred communication styles within online cancer communities: A retrospective, longitudinal analysis. *Plos One*, 7, 1-11. doi: 10.1371/journal.pone.0049169.

Eichhorn, K. C. (2008). Soliciting and providing social support over the Internet: An investigation of online eating disorder support groups. *Journal of Computer-Mediated Communication*, 14, 67-78. doi: 10.1111/j.1083-6101.2008.01431.x.

Feng, B. (2009). Testing an integrated model of advice giving in supportive interactions. *Human Communication Research*, 35, 115-129. doi: 10.1111/j.1468-2958.2008.01340.x.

Feng, B., and Hyun, M. J. (2012). The influence of friends' instant messenger status on individuals' coping and support-seeking. *Communication Studies*, 63, 536-553. doi: 10.1080/10510974.2011.649443.

Feng, B., Li, S., and Li, N. (2016). Is a profile worth a thousand words?: How online support-seeker's profile features may influence the quality of received support messages. *Communication Research*, 43(2), 253-276. doi: 10.1177/0093650213510942.

Ginossar, T. (2008). Online participation: A content analysis of differences in utilization of two online cancer communities by men and women, patients and family members. *Health Communication*, 23, 1-12. doi: 10. 1080/10410230701697100.

Griffith, J. (1985). Social support providers: Who are they? Where are they met? and the relationship of network characteristics to psychological distress. *Basic and Applied Social Psychology*, 6, 41-60. doi: 10.1207/ s15324834basp0601_4.

Griffiths, K. M., Calear, A. L., and Banfield, M. (2009). Systematic review on internet support groups (ISGs) and depression (1): Do ISGs reduce depressive symptoms? *Journal of Medical Internet Research*, 11, 1-20.

High, A. C., Oeldorf-Hirsch, A., and Bellur, S. (2014). Misery rarely gets company: The influence of emotional bandwidth on supportive communication on Facebook. *Computers in Human Behavior*, 34, 79- 88. doi: 10.1016/j.chb.2014.01.037.

Li, S., and Feng, B. (2015). What to say to an online support-seeker?: The influence of others' responses and support-seekers' replies. *Human Communication Research*, 41, 303-326.

Lee, E-J., and Jang, J-W. (2013). Not so imaginary interpersonal contact with public figures on social network sites: How affiliative tendency moderates its effects. *Communication Research*, 40, 27-51.

Lee, K. M., and Nass, C. (2005). Social-psychological origins of feelings of presence: Creating social presence with machine-generated voices. *Media Psychology*, 7, 31-45.

Lewandowski, J., Rosenberg, B. D., Jordan Parks, M., and Siegel, J. T. (2011). The effect of informal social support: Face-to-face versus computer-mediated communication. *Computers in Human Behavior*,

27, 1806-1814. doi: http://dx.doi.org/10.1016/j.chb.2011.03.008.

MacGeorge, E. L., Feng, B., and Thompson, E. R. (2008). "Good" and "bad" advice: How to advise more effectively. In: M. T. Motley, ed., *Studies in Applied Interpersonal Communication*. Thousand Oaks, CA: Sage, pp. 145-164.

MacGeorge, E. L., Feng, B., and Burleson, B. R. (2011). Supportive communication. In: M. L. Knapp, and J. A. Daly, eds., *Handbook of Interpersonal Communication*. Thousand Oaks, CA: Sage, pp. 317-354.

McMahon, G. T., Gomes, H. E., Hickson Hohne, S., Hu, T. M., Levine, B. A., and Conlin, P. R. (2005). Web-based care management in patients with poorly controlled diabetes. *Diabetes Care*, 28, 1624-1629.

Mesch, G. S., and Beker, G. (2010). Are norms of disclosure of online and offline personal information associated with the disclosure of personal information online? *Human Communication Research*, 36, 570-592. doi: 10.1111/j.1468-2958.2010.01389.x.

Metzger, M. J., and Flanagin, A. J. (2011). Using Web 2.0 technologies to enhance evidence-based medical information. *J Health Commun*, 16, suppl 1, 45-58. doi: 10.1080/10810730.2011.589881.

Mikal, J. P., Rice, R. E., Abeyta, A., and DeVilbiss, J. (2013). Transition, stress and computer-mediated social support. *Computers in Human Behavior*, 29, A40-A53. doi: http://dx.doi.org/10.1016/j.chb.2012.12.012.

Oh, H. J., Ozkaya, E., and LaRose, R. (2014). How does online social networking enhance life satisfaction?: The relationships among online supportive interaction, affect, perceived social support, sense of community, and life satisfaction. *Computers in Human Behavior*, 30, 69-78. doi: http://dx.doi.org/10.1016/j.chb.2013.07.053.

O'Sullivan, P. B., and Carr, C. T. (2018). Masspersonal communication: A model bridging the mass-interpersonal divide. *New Media & Society*, 20(3), 1161-1180. doi: 10.1177/1461444816686104.

Petty, R. E., and Cacioppo, J. T. (1986). *Communication and persuasion: Central and peripheral routes to attitude change*. New York: Springer-Verlag.

Petty, R. E., and Wegener, D. T. (1999). The elaboration likelihood model: Current status and controversies. In: S. Chaiken, and Y. Trope, eds., *Dual Process Theories in Social Psychology*. New York: Guilford Press, pp. 41-72.

Rains, S. A. (2013). The Implications of stigma and anonymity for self-disclosure in health blogs. *Health Communication*, 29, 23-31. doi: 10.1080/10410236.2012.714861.

Rains, S. A., and Keating, D. M. (2011). The social dimension of blogging about health: Health blogging, social support, and well-being. *Communication Monographs*, 78, 511-534. doi: 10.1080/0363 7751.2011.618142.

Rains, S. A., and Keating, D. M. (2015). Health blogging: An examination of the outcomes associated with making public, written disclosures about health. *Communication Research*, 42(1), 107-133. doi: 10.1177/0093 650212458952.

Rains, S. A., Peterson, E. B., and Wright, K. B. (2015). Communicating social support in computer-mediated contexts: A meta-analytic review of content analyses examining support messages shared online among individuals coping with illness. *Communication Monographs*, 82(4), 403-430. doi: 10.1080/03637751.2015.1019530.

Rains, S. A., and Young, V. (2009). A meta-analysis of research on formal computer-mediated support groups: Examining group characteristics and health outcomes. *Human Communication Research*, 35, 309-336. doi: 10.1111/j.1468-2958.2009.01353.x.

Robinson, J. D., Turner, J. W., Levine, B., and Tian, Y. (2011). Expanding the walls of the health care encounter: Support and outcomes for patients online. *Health Communication*, 26, 125-134. doi: 10.1080/ 10410236.2010.541990.

Shaw, B. R. , Hawkins, R. , McTavish, F. , Pingree, S. , and Gustafson, D. H. (2006). Effects of insightful disclosure within computer mediated support groups on women with breast cancer. *Health Communication*, 19, 133-142. doi: 10.1207/s15327027hc1902_5.

Short, J. , Williams, E. , and Christie, B. (1976). *The Social Psychology of Telecommunication*. London: John Wiley.

Spottswood, E. L. , Walther, J. B. , Holmstrom, A. J. , and Ellison, N. B. (2013). Person-centered emotional support and gender attributions in computer-mediated communication. *Human Communication Research*, 39, 295-316. doi: 10.1111/hcre.12006.

Tanis, M. (2008). Health-related on-line forums: What's the big attraction? *Journal of Health Communication*, 13, 698-714. doi: 10.1080/108107 30802415316.

Tichon, J. G. , and Shapiro, M. (2003). The process of sharing social support in cyberspace. *Cyberpsychology & Behavior*, 6, 161-170. doi: 10.1089/109493103321640356.

Turner, J. W. , Grube, J. A. , and Meyers, J. (2001). Developing an optimal match within online communities: An exploration of CMC support communities and traditional support. *Journal of Communication*, 51, 231-251. doi: 10.1111/j.1460-2466.2001.tb02879.x.

Turner, J. W. , Robinson, J. D. , Tian, Y. , Neustadtl, A. , Angelus, P. , Russell, M. , and Levine, B. (2013). Can messages make a difference?: The association between e-mail messages and health outcomes in diabetes patients. *Human Communication Research*, 39(2), 252-268. doi: 10.1111/j.1468-2958.2012.01437.x.

VanLear, C. A. , Sheehan, M. , Withers, L. A. , and Walker, R. A. (2005). AA online: The enactment of supportive Computer Mediated Communication. *Western Journal of Communication*, 69, 5-26. doi: 10.1080/10570310500033941.

Walther, J. B. (1992). Interpersonal effects in computer-mediated interaction: A relational perspective. *Communication Research*, 19, 52-90.

Walther, J. B. (1996). Computer-mediated communication: Impersonal, interpersonal, and hyperpersonal interaction. *Communication Research*, 23, 3-43.

Walther, J. B. (1997). Group and interpersonal effects in international computer-mediated collaboration. *Human Communication Research*, 23, 342-369. doi: 10.1111/j.1468-2958.1997.tb00400.x.

Walther, J. B., and Boyd, S. (2002). Attraction to computer-mediated social support. In: C. A. Lin and D. Atkin, eds., *Communication Technology and Society: Audience Adoption and Uses*. Cresskill, NJ: Hampton Press, pp. 153-188.

Walther, J. B., and Parks, M. R. (2002). Cues filtered out, cues filtered in: Computer-mediated communication and relationships. In: M. L. Knapp, and J. A. Daly, eds., *Handbook of Interpersonal Communication*. 3rd ed. Thousand Oaks, CA: Sage, pp. 529-563.

Wang, Z., Walther, J. B., Pingree, S., and Hawkins, R. P. (2008). Health information, credibility, homophily, and influence via the Internet: Web sites versus discussion groups. *Health Commun*, 23, 358-368. doi: 10.1080/10410230802229738.

White, M., and Dorman, S. M. (2001). Receiving social support online: Implications for health education. *Health Education Research*, 16, 693-707. doi: 10.1093/her/16.6.693.

Womble, L. G., Wadden, T. A., McGuckin, B. G., Sargent, S. L., Rothman, R. A., and Krauthamer-Ewing, E. S. (2004). A randomized controlled trial of a commercial Internet weight loss program. *Obesity Research*, 12, 1011-1018. doi: 10.1038/oby.2004.124.

Wright, K. (2000). Perceptions of on-line support providers: An examination of perceived homophily, source credibility, communication and social support within on-line support groups. *Communication Quarterly*, 48, 44-59.

Wright, K. (2002). Social support within an on-line cancer community: An assessment of emotional support, perceptions of advantages and disadvantages, and motives for using the community from a communication perspective. *Journal of Applied Communication Research*, 30, 195-209. doi: 10.1080/00909880216586.

Wright, K. B., and Bell, S. B. (2003). Health-related support groups on the Internet: Linking empirical findings to social support and computer-mediated communication theory. *Journal of Health Psychology*, 8, 39-54. doi: 10.1177/1359105303008001429.

Wright, K. B., Rains, S., and Banas, J. (2010). Weak-tie support network preference and perceived life stress among participants in health-related, computer-mediated support groups. *Journal of Computer-Mediated Communication*, 15, 606-624. doi: 10.1111/j.1083-6101.2009.01505.x.

Wright, K. B., and Rains, S. A. (2014). Weak tie support preference and preferred coping styles as predictors of perceived credibility within health-related computer-mediated support groups. *Health Communication*, 29, 281-287. doi: 10.1080/10410236.2012.751084.

Wright, K. B., Rosenberg, J., Egbert, N., Ploeger, N. A., Bernard, D. R., and King, S. (2013). Communication competence, social support, and depression among college students: A model of Facebook and face-to-face support network influence. *Journal of Health Communication*, 18, 41-57. doi: 10.1080/10810730.2012.688250.

Chapter 2　Other-Generated Comments and Online Support Provision

Social support can facilitate individuals' coping with stressful events and enhance individuals' physical and psychological well-being (MacGeorge, Feng, Burleson, 2011). While people primarily seek support from personal relationships, especially close relationships (Feng & Burleson, 2006; Uchino, 2004), seeking help from unknown others has become increasingly common with the advancement of new technologies (Blank et al., 2010; Coulson, Buchanan, Aubeeluck, 2007; Xie, 2008).[1]

As a popular avenue of support exchange, online support forums have received increasing interests in communication research (Rains & Young, 2009; Walther & Boyd, 2002; Wright & Bell, 2003). These forums are largely free of temporal and spatial constraints, allowing individuals to seek support online at their convenience while at the same time enhancing their opportunity to meet others with similar experiences (Tichon & Shapiro, 2003). Further, the anonymous feature of the vast majority of online communication among strangers affords people an enhanced sense of security (Fullwood & Wootton, 2009; Tanis, 2008) and facilitates self-disclosure in supportive interaction (Barak, Boniel-Nissim, Suler, 2008; Fullwood & Wootton, 2009). Past research has shown that online support can have a profound impact on personal health, including decreased depression, enhanced quality of life, and higher efficacy to manage one's health condition (Rains & Young, 2009).

Despite the impressive body of literature on this topic, online supportive communication remains a fledgling area. To date, the majority of studies on online support have focused on investigating predictors (e. g. , personality traits and motivations) (Wright, 2000) or outcomes (e. g. , physical and psychological health) (Rains & Young, 2009) of online support-seeking rather than the actual message production in supportive communication (Feng, Li, Li, 2016). Further, online supportive has been studied primarily through constant analyses and surveys which offer limited insights on causality among different factors. This study attempts to fill these gaps by presenting an experiment to study interactions among online support-seekers and support-providers. Specifically, it looks at how earlier comments on a support-seeking post and a support-seeker's response to these comments will affect subsequent viewers' impression of and response to the support-seeker. In the remainder of this chapter, the author first provids an overview of the key constructs and outlined hypotheses in relation to the theoretical foundations, and then presents an empirical experiment, followed by discussions of the results.

2.1 Quality of Support Messages: Person-Centeredness

It is a well-established assumption in research on supportive communication that there are qualitative differences in the support messages that people give and receive (MacGeorge et al. , 2004). Some forms of support messages are more effective than others in comforting distressed individuals and helping them to solve problems. The quality of support messages has been theoretically differentiated by person-centeredness, which refers to "an awareness of and adaption to the subjective, affective, and relational aspects of communicative contexts" (Burleson, 1987). Past research on supportive communication has prioritized the emotional and cognitive aspects of person-centeredness by examining the extent to which a message explicitly validates a person's feelings and provides a different perspective to appraise the target's situation (Burleson & Goldsmith, 1998). In this study, we argue that, besides the emotional and cognitive aspects of a target's situation, person-centered support messages should also tap into the dimensions of the target's behaviors and face concerns. Therefore, we propose a three-dimension construct of person-centeredness in supportive communication, including emotion-focused supportiveness, action-focused supportiveness, and politeness.

2. 1. 1 Emotion-Focused Supportiveness

Emotional support has long been recognized as an effective means to comfort distressed others. Research suggests that people generally benefit from emotional support across different situations (Burleson, 2003). The traditional measurement of verbal person-centeredness focuses on this dimension (MacGeorge, Feng, Burleson, 2011). In Burleson's (1982) hierarchy of person-centeredness, low person-centered comforting support messages are operationalized as those that deny or ignore the feelings of a recipient, messages displaying moderate level of person-centeredness convey an implicit recognition of the other's feelings, and highly person-centered comforting messages explicitly recognize and legitimize the recipient's feelings. This measurement has been widely applied in studies of emotional support, and substantial evidence shows that comforting messages exhibiting high person-centeredness tend to be viewed as more effective than those exhibiting lower levels of person-centeredness (for a review, see High & Dillard, 2012).

2. 1. 2 Action-Focused Supportiveness

Action-focused supportiveness is conceptualized in this study as the extent to which a helper legitimizes, shows understanding of, or endorses a support-seeker's enacted or intended course of action. Research shows that criticizing someone's enacted behavior may arouse or exacerbate negative

35

affect in the recipient and may trigger the recipient's negative perceptions of the self (Cupach & Carson, 2002; Wagoner & Waldron, 1999). There is also evidence indicating that when individuals' behaviors are endorsed by others, they tend to experience more positive affect and appraisal of themselves (Kamins & Dweck, 1999). With regard to intended behaviors, the extent to which a helper suggests an action in accordance with a recipient's intention has been identified as a notable aspect of support messages (MacGeorge, Feng, Thompson, 2008). This notion of confirmation is consistent with the propositions of social judgment theory (Sherif & Hovland, 1961), which suggests that people are more likely to be persuaded by messages that approximate their initial attitudes. For instance, Yaniv (2004) found in a series of studies that people placed more weight on advice that was more proximate to their initial opinions. More directly relevant is Feng and MacGeorge's (2010) study showing that advice recipient's perception of the extent to which a piece of advice confirms the recipient's intended behavior positively influences the recipient's evaluations of advice quality, facilitation of coping, and intention to implement the advice. Despite empirical evidence in support of the notion that action-focused supportiveness is an indicator of support messages' quality, the current study is, to our knowledge, the first to explicitly classify this aspect as a dimension of support messages.

2.1.3 Politeness

The third dimension of person-centeredness pertains to face concerns in supportive communication. Face is an inherent concern within the complexity of supportive communication (Aakhus & Rumsey, 2010; Goldsmith, 1992). Politeness theory (Brown & Levinson, 1987; Goffman, 2003) categorizes people's face needs into two types: positive face and negative face. Positive face refers to individuals' desire to maintain a favorable self-image and obtain approval from others, especially those in personal relationships.

Negative face relates to the need to maintain one's autonomy without imposition from others. Politeness theory suggests that people are concerned about their own faces as well as others' faces. When the face is under threat, two types of politeness strategies can be employed to mitigate the threat: positive politeness and negative politeness. Positive politeness acknowledges the positive images of the target and negative politeness attempts to minimize imposition on the target's autonomy and freedom of choice.

In supportive interactions, disclosing problems and expressing distress inevitably threaten support-seekers' positive face as they reveal their weaknesses (e. g. , lack of competence in managing problems) to others. Seeking support from others also challenges support-seekers' negative face as receiving support from others may create imposition on recipients' autonomy of thinking and behaving (e. g. , a support-seeker may feel obligated to implement a piece of advice or reciprocate the favor in the future). The aforementioned concerns over face may exacerbate support-seekers' negative emotions and lower their confidence to effectively cope with their problems (Goldsmith, 1994). Attending to support-seekers' face needs can thus help to alleviate their stress and facilitate their problem solving (MacGeorge et al. , 2004). In fact, there is ample research evidence that support messages attentive to recipients' face needs are evaluated more favorably than those that fail to address face concerns (Goldsmith & MacGeorge, 2000; MacGeorge et al. , 2004).

As theory of constructivism and prior research on social support suggest, the production of person-centered messages requires both capacity and motivation (Burleson, 1987, 2003). Besides variation in cognitive capacity, people also differ in their motivation to produce high-quality support messages. For example, research suggests that attribution of a support-seeker's responsibility tends to influence a helper's motivation to provide high-quality emotional support (MacGeorge, 2001). Recent research on online supportive communication suggests that readers' perceptions of an online support-seeker, such as the support-seeker's social presence and trustworthiness, may enhance their motivation to provide higher quality support messages (Feng, Li, Li, 2016). The current study tests the idea that others' responses to a support-seeking post may influence a reader's inclination to provide more or less person-centered support messages through two mechanisms which are explained in the following sections.

2.2 Online Comments and Perceived Supportiveness in Public Opinion

Traditional mass media such as television are typically characterized as low-interactive media because messages are linearly delivered to audiences without much feedback (Schultz, 2000). The absence of direct access to public opinion leads audiences to rely heavily on dominant viewpoints regarding an issue shown in traditional mass media to infer public climate. With the emergence of the Internet, the interactive nature of online communication has significantly changed communication dynamics. Unlike audiences of traditional media, online users are empowered to express their opinions in cyberspace that are often readily visible to others. These user-generated comments may be perceived as representing public opinion and allow audiences to directly assess the public climate regarding a certain issue. For instance, research on online news shows that others' comments on an issue tend to exert greater influence on people's perceptions of public opinion than does news article itself (Lee & Jang, 2010).

The inferred public opinion based on others' comments is likely to influence audience's reactions to the issue under discussion. Extant literature suggests that the motivation of being correct drives people to engage in social comparison which enables them to ascertain and adopt the most predominant opinions (Festinger, 1950). User-generated comments provide information about other people's thoughts, from which an individual can assess the predominant opinion and thus the most acceptable and appropriate judgment for the individual to hold (Fein, Goethals, Kugler,

2007).

On support forums, a support-seeking post may elicit a number of responses. Although some readers may show support and sympathy to the support-seeker, others may think the support-seeker is blameworthy for his or her distressing situation. Flaming and hostile communication may also appear on support forums (Aakhus & Rumsey, 2010; White & Dorman, 2001). Given the lack of knowledge about and familiarity with an unknown support-seeker, others' comments can function as an important heuristic cue (Metzger, Flanagin, Medders, 2010) to help readers infer public opinion regarding the focal issue, which in turn can affect readers' reactions to the support-seeker. In other words, the predominant position toward a support-seeker, which is reflected in others' comments, may be perceived by subsequent readers as the appropriate position to adopt and thereby influence the readers' inclination to provide more or less person-centered responses. If earlier responses predominantly support a support-seeker, a reader may perceive the public opinion to be supportive, and therefore be motivated to provide a response exhibiting a relatively high level of person-centeredness. As aforementioned, person-centeredness of support messages will be assessed in this study along three dimensions: emotion-focused supportiveness, action-focused supportiveness, and politeness. The extent to which these three features are instantiated in a reader's support message is expected to be affected by the perceived supportiveness in public opinion. Therefore, the following hypothesis is proposed.

H1: Compared to readers exposed to unsupportive comments on a support-seeker's posting, those exposed to supportive comments will perceive the public opinion to be more supportive of the support-seeker and will in turn provide responses with (a) higher level of emotion-focused supportiveness, (b) higher level of action-focused supportiveness, and (c) greater use of politeness strategies.

2.3 Online Comments and Impression Formation

Besides the mediating role of perceived public opinion, impression formation may function through a concurrent mechanism underlying the link between others' comments and a reader's response. Consciously or subconsciously, readers will form impression of a support-seeker when reading the support-seeker's post and any existing responses from others (Walther et al., 2008; Walther et al., 2009). Due to the absence of many nonverbal cues and lack of prior knowledge about an online support-seeker, people have very limited information (i.e., the support-seeker's self-generated information, such as their support-seeking post and profile picture) to form an impression of the support-seeker. Therefore, other cues available on the site provide additional information to assist a reader's judgment of the target (Walther et al., 2008).

Brunswik's (1956) lens model provides a useful framework for examining impression formation on support forums. According to the model, individuals' behaviors and surrounding artifacts are indicators of their characteristics. Observers rely on both behaviors and environmental cues to infer characteristics of others. Gosling and his colleagues (Gosling et al., 2002) extended this model by proposing two types of cues that link individuals to their inhabiting environments: identity claims and behavioral residue. Identity claims are symbols intentionally displayed by an individual to present his/her personal identity, whereas behavioral residues that reflect past or further behaviors are physical traces of activities performed by the individual or others.

Although Brunswik's (1959) lens model and Gosling et al.'s (2002) extension of the model were originally designed to examine impression formation in physical space, they have been applied to understand impression formation in cyberspace (Antheunis & Schouten, 2011). On participatory websites, including support forums, both identity claims and behavioral residues are present. Identity claims in support forums include support-seeker's profile and postings, as well as other information within the control of a support-seeker. Behavioral residues include earlier posts by the same support-seeker and responses left by other readers. Despite their exemption from a support-seeker's manipulation, other readers' responses are results of the support-seeker's behavior (i. e. , soliciting support online) and can thus serve as useful cues in impression formation of the support-seeker.

Research on participatory websites has largely validated the role of others' comments in impression formation of a profile owner (Antheunis & Schouten, 2011; Edwards & Edwards, 2013). For instance, Walther and his colleagues (2009) found that observers rely heavily on friend-generated statements on Facebook to judge a profile owner's physical attractiveness. Edwards and his associates (Edwards et al. , 2007; Edwards & Edwards, 2013) conducted a series of studies on www. ratemyprofessors. com to examine the influence of others' comments on evaluation of an instructor. They found that students who read positive comments evaluated the instructor to be more credible and attractive than those who read negative comments. With limited information available about a support-seeker online, readers may utilize the behavioral residues such as others' responses to form impression of the support-seeker. Although impression can be assessed from different dimensions (e. g. , physical attractiveness, trust, liking), the author chose to focus on liking of a support-seeker because of its salience in online communication (Walther & Bunz, 2005) and its particular relevance to the manipulations in this study (i. e. , comments from readers who do not know the support-seeker). Among different dimensions of impression, liking is a salient one in a variety of communication contexts (Collins & Miller, 1994; Goei et al. , 2003). For example, people tend to self-disclose more to likeable others (Collins & Miller, 1994). Research on persuasion reveals that increased liking of a favor requester tends to lead to more compliance (Goei et al. , 2003). In addition, people are less likely to exhibit aggressive behaviors toward liked others than disliked others (Lott & Lott, 1965). On support forums, viewers' liking of a support-seeker may affect how they respond to a support-seeking post.

More specifically, it is predicted that if a majority of respondents show sympathy and support to the support-seeker, a reader will perceive the support-seeker to be more likable. Liking can in turn motivate a reader to produce more supportive response to the support-seeker. In contrast, unsupportive comments from others may lead to less liking of the support-seeker and thus lower motivation to offer high-quality support. Accordingly, the following hypothesis is proposed.

H2: Compared to readers exposed to unsupportive comments on a support-seeker's posting, those exposed to supportive comments will perceive the support-seeker to be more likable and will in turn provide responses with (a) higher level of emotion-focused supportiveness, (b) higher level of action-focused supportiveness, and (c) greater use of politeness strategies (Figure 2.1).

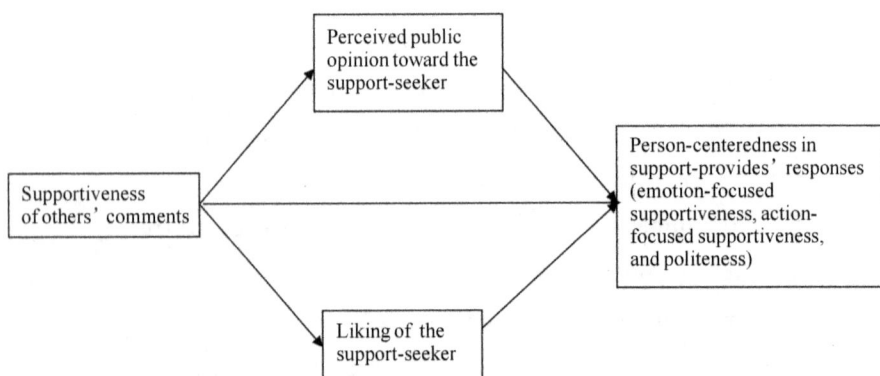

Figure 2.1   Masspersonal model of support provision online

2.4 Support-Seeker's Reply

The interactive environment on participatory websites allows direct communication among their users. An individual's reply to others' comments can serve as identity claim and potentially influence readers' perceptions of him or her. For instance, an online seller's apology to consumers' complaints can be more effective than a denial in restoring trust in the seller (Matzat & Snijders, 2012). On support forums, whether or not a support-seeker expresses appreciation of others' responses may affect a reader's liking toward the support-seeker. However, the interplay between valence of a support-seeker's reply and others' comments may complicate the process of forming impression of a support-seeker. For example, expressing gratitude to unsupportive comments might be perceived as being either sincere or hypocritical. To date, no study has investigated how the support-seeker's reply and others' comments interact and affect a reader's response to a support-seeking post. Therefore, the following research question is raised.

RQ: Will a support-seeker's reply to others' comments influence a reader's perception of the support-seeker's likability or the quality of support message?

2.5 Hypotheses Testing with an Experiment

2.5.1 Participants

Data were collected from students who registered in communication classes at a large west coast university in the United States. IRB (Institutional Review Board) approval was obtained prior to subject recruitment and data collection. Participants were recruited through an in-class announcement and they signed up on a volunteer basis at the beginning or end of a class period. Respondents were offered a small amount of extra credit for participating in the study. A total of 390 undergraduate students participated in the study. Responses to the support-seeking post from 29 participants were not successfully saved and these participants were excluded from subsequent analyses. 4 additional participants were dropped because their online survey data were not successfully saved, leaving a total of 357 participants in the final analysis (146 male, 211 female). The majority of the participants were Asian American (63.0%, $n = 225$) and Caucasian (20.7%, $n = 74$), but the sample also included Hispanic Americans (8.7%, $n = 31$), African Americans (3.4%, $n = 12$), and other ethnicity groups (4.2%, $n = 14$).[2]

2.5.2 Design

This study employed a 2 (others' comments: supportive vs. unsupportive) × 3 (seeker's reply to others' comments: no reply vs. appreciative reply vs. inappreciative reply) × 2 (problem topics: roommate conflict vs. internship) factorial design. The interface of a real online forum "forums. student. com" was utilized in this study.[3] This design differed from previous studies on computer-mediated communication that typically used a mock-up web page as the stimuli (Walther et al. , 2008). As discussed earlier, using the interface of a real-existing online support forum allows researchers to examine online supportive communication in a more ecologically valid manner.

To enhance external validity, two topics that pertain to college students' life were used. In one post, the support-seeker talked about having conflicting schedule with a roommate. The support-seeker wanted to study in the room with a desk light on after 11 pm whereas the roommate insisted that the support-seeker turn off the desk light at 11 pm. The other post involved an internship issue, in which the support-seeker complained about doing manual work and not being respected by the boss, leading to the support-seeker's inclination to quit.

To manipulate the supportiveness of others' comments on the original post, two sets of comments differing in valence were created for each topic. Each set of comments contained eight responses exclusively being supportive or unsupportive. For example, a positive comment on the roommate topic was "I back you up! You have a room to live in, so why can't you be in it? If someone is sleeping that early, he/she gotta learn to tolerate the roommate—it's not his/her room only." An example of negative comments on this topic was "Just fix your studying schedule man… or find another place to study. That room belongs to your roommate too, so it'll be inconsiderate to ask him to fix his sleeping schedule for you." Efforts were made to keep the length and reading levels of the two versions for each comment set comparable.

The manipulation of support-seeker's reply to others' comments included three conditions: appreciative reply (i.e., "Thank you so much! I really appreciate all your input! 😊"), inappreciative reply (i.e., "I want to get more input"), and no reply. The support-seeker's reply was always displayed beneath the eighth comment. All other visible features of the support-seeking post (e.g., user ID, profile) were held constant across experimental conditions.

2. 5. 3 Procedure

Upon arrival at the research lab, each participant was randomly assigned to an experimental condition and escorted by a research assistant to a cubicle with a laptop. Participants were instructed to create a username and respond to the support-seeker after reading the original post and subsequent comments. After clicking the button "post a reply," the participant's response would appear immediately underneath the set of manipulated comments (and support-seeker's reply, if applicable). Each participant was only able to view his or her own response; that is, other participants' submitted responses would not be displayed on the screen. After submitting their responses, participants were directed to the survey system "Qualtrics" to complete a survey on their perceptions and opinions regarding the issue and the support-seeker.[3] Upon completion of the survey, participants were thanked and debriefed.

2. 5. 4 Measures

Perceived supportiveness in public opinion. Six items on a 7-point scale (1 = *strongly disagree*, 7 = *strongly agree*) were created based on a couple existing measures (Lee, 2012; Shoemaker, Breen, Stamper, 2000) to assess perceived supportiveness in public opinion toward the support-seeker with regard to the focal issue. Sample items include "The public will sympathize with the support-seeker" and "The public will be supportive to the support-seeker if they respond to the original posting." The scale exhibited high internal consistency ($M = 4.31$, $SD = 1.38$, $\alpha = 0.92$).

Liking of the support-seeker. A scale of six items on a 7-point scale (1 = *strongly disagree*, 7 = *strongly agree*) modified from Rubin's (1970) liking scale was used to measure participants' liking toward the support-seeker. Examples of the items are "The support-seeker seems to be a likable person" and "The support-seeker sounds like a friendly person." The items manifested a high reliability ($M = 4.23$, $SD = 1.11$, $\alpha = 0.96$).

Coding for emotion-focused supportiveness. One author and an undergraduate research assistant coded emotion-focused supportiveness of participants' responses. The coding scheme was adapted from the hierarchy of person-centeredness (Burleson, 1982) and the emotion-focused coding system was developed by Jones and Burleson (1996). Each message was coded into one of the nine sublevels embedded in the three major levels (Table 2.1). Messages that deny the recipient's feelings by criticizing, challenging, or ignoring them were coded within Level 1. Messages that implicitly acknowledge the recipient's feelings by conveying hope, expressing sympathy, or providing explanation of the situation were coded within Level 2. Messages that explicitly recognize the recipient's feelings and help the recipient to reappraise the situation from a different perceptive were coded within Level 3. A message that represents more than one sublevel was coded by its dominant level. The two coders independently coded an overlapping 30% of the messages ($n = 105$). Krippendorff's alpha for coding agreement was 0.70. Disagreements were resolved through discussions. The undergraduate assistant then coded the remaining data.

Table 2.1　Emotion-focused supportiveness coding hierarchy and examples

Levels of emotion-focused supportiveness	Definitions and examples
Level 1	Speaker explicitly criticizes, condemns, or challenges the target's feelings or characters.
	Example: Don't be so childish! Either study in the library like everyone else or stop being such a drama queen and talk to your roommate about it.
Level 2	Speaker criticizes the target's behaviors or supports the other party's behaviors, feelings, or characters.
	Example: You've only been there for a week and you've already been late for work? Seriously? No wonder you can only do menial tasks.
Level 3	Speaker ignores the target's feelings or asks the target to ignore his/her feelings.
	Example: Shake it off. Maybe you should go and talk to your boss.

Continued

Levels of emotion-focused supportiveness	Definitions and examples
Level 4	Speaker suggests or implies that the target may feel better about the situation or the situation may improve at some point in the future.
	Example: You should stick it out for a while. It has only been a week, so there are chances that it will improve. Always try to make the most out of any experience. Even if it does not turn out to be so great, it can prepare you for the real world. Hope things get better :)
Level 5	Speaker expresses sympathy, understanding, or condolence without providing any legitimization or explanation of the target's feelings.
	Example: I completely understand your predicament; I can't study very well before 10 p.m. either. I would just suggest being assertive with him and letting him know how important this is to you.
Level 6	Speaker provides a non-feeling-centered explanation of the situation or attempts to help the target to reappraise the situation in order to reduce the target's distressed emotional state.
	Example: This is exactly what I am afraid of when I do intern work. I feel like I will be given irrelevant tasks that do not even relate to the position and just be treated like a slave. I know interning is supposed to look good on your resume, so you should probably just stay so you can have experience, and it will look better on your resume. But if you really cannot handle it after another week or so, then you should quit. This always seems to be a problem with internships in that you either are given too much information to learn or too little.

Continued

Levels of emotion-focused supportiveness	Definitions and examples
Level 7	Speaker provides an explicit legitimization of the target's feelings.
	Example: You should talk to your roommate and collaborate for a win-win situation. Make sure they understand that you are also living in this room. I do agree on how you feel about it though; that is very frustrating and the other roommate is quite selfish. Maybe suggest you guys hang up a curtain or something? I can't really sleep with lights on either but what I do is using a sleeping mask to cover my eyes and that works perfectly well. Don't approach the situation negatively though! Try to work things out because you DO live with this person.
Level 8	Speaker explicitly acknowledges the target's feelings and provides an elaborated explanation of those feelings.
	Example: I can understand how you feel—I'm a late sleeper myself. If you're looking for advice I'd say try to create an alternative study area for yourself maybe in the living room or kitchen area. Obviously it's going to be very difficult for you to study while someone wants the room dark. So instead of wasting your time and energy being upset about the situation, use the time and energy to solve the issue. In life, nothing will be perfect and adaptability is very important. So start now, friend!

Continued

Levels of emotion-focused supportiveness	Definitions and examples
	Speaker helps the target to gain a perspective on his/her own feelings (feelings in the situation are explicitly recognized and legitimized/explained) and attempts to help the target to reappraise the situation, in order to reduce the target's distressed emotional state.
Level 9	*Example: Dear eye111111, I understand where you are coming from. If anyone was treated with such disrespect at work, I would feel disappointed, and want to quit right on the spot. However, instead of resulting with the final solution of quitting, I think you should try to save your internship first. First, try to confront your supervisor. Ask him why you were given only menial tasks, as if you haven't yet. Ask him why you were only given menial tasks, as well as why you were given no specific suggestions. Let him know you feel disappointed and offended, provided that it won't lead to greater problems. Also, let him know that you at least deserve an explanation. If you really value your internship, you should at least try to save it before quitting. I just hope that your supervisor does not ignore your confrontation, and works with you in solving the conflict that you two have. Sincerely, Edean91*

Coding for action-focused supportiveness. A nine-level hierarchy of action-focused supportiveness was created based, in part, on the problem-focused coding system developed by Jones and Burleson (1996) (Table 2.2). The degree of supportiveness regarding the target's action increases with each level. The first four levels represent unsupportive positions. The fifth level is the middle point which stands for a neutral position toward the supper-seeker's action. The last there levels represent supportive positions. Actions were categorized into enacted actions (actions that the target has already performed) and intended actions (actions that the target intends to perform). This distinction is made to account for the possibility that a helper supports the target's intended action but not an enacted action, or vice versa. The hierarchy is separately applied to each type of actions. The same coders coded the participants' response messages. In order to assess inter-coder reliability, both coders coded an overlapping 32% ($n = 115$) of participants' support messages. Krippendorff's alpha for coding agreement were 0.75 and 0.87 for supportiveness of enacted and intended actions, respectively. Coding discrepancies were resolved through discussion. The undergraduate research assistant coded the rest of the messages.

Table 2.2　Action-focused supportiveness coding hierarchy and examples

Levels of action-focused supportiveness	Definitions and examples
Level 1	Speaker expresses intention to punish the target for an enacted behavior or prevent the target from performing the target's intended behavior.
	Example: If you keep complaining here, I will let your roommate know and he will never allow you to study in the room.
Level 2	Speaker criticizes or condemns the target's enacted or intended behavior.
	Example: You are definitely acting entitled. You can't have everything that you want. You just started your internship. Can't you be a little patient?
Level 3	Speaker explicitly endorses a behavior that contradicts with the target's enacted or intended behavior.
	Example: Sounds pretty typical for an internship. You have to be patient and be willing to put more effort in to get anything out of it.

Continued

Levels of action-focused supportiveness	Definitions and examples
Level 4	Speaker implicitly endorses a behavior that contradicts with the target's enacted or intended behavior.
	Example: I stay up late but never in the room. If I'm on the computer at my desk and my roommate goes to bed I'll turn off the lights and go to the living room. If I stayed in there with lights on I know I'd deserve to be complained about.
Level 5	Speaker expresses a neutral position pertaining to the target's enacted or intended behavior.
	Example: You should be able to study at the hours you want to, but your roommate should also be able to sleep when he needs to without too much distraction. Work with your roommate to find a solution that leaves both of you satisfied. Perhaps you can find a study area on campus that suits you, or perhaps your roommate can wear a sleeping mask to block out the light for your lamp. The best resolution is going to need input from both parties.
Level 6	Speaker implicitly endorses the target's enacted or intended behavior.
	Example: I can definitely relate to you. I did an internship where the advisor didn't care about the interns. He never listened to me... so I quitted the internship three weeks later.
Level 7	Speaker explicitly endorses the target's enacted or intended behavior.
	Example: I'm sorry to hear that about your internship. I'm sure you can find a better internship where your boss can be more respectful and you will actually enjoy what you do.
Level 8	Speaker explicitly endorses and praises the target's enacted or intended behavior.
	Example: I will be very proud of you if you quit the job!

Continued

Levels of action-focused supportiveness	Definitions and examples
Level 9	Speaker offers to strengthen or award the target's enacted behavior or provide assistance to the target in order to help the target perform the target's intended behavior.
	Example: I can definitely relate to you. I did an internship where the advisor didn't care about the interns. He never listened to me... so I quitted the internship three weeks later. If you need information on how to find a new internship without burning bridge with your current one, feel free to send me a private message.

Coding for politeness. The coding scheme developed by Feng, Li and Li (2016) based on Brown and Levinson's work (1987) on politeness strategies was adapted and modified for use in this study. The coding scheme included twelve positive and seven negative politeness strategies (see Tables 2.3 & 2.4). Two undergraduate research assistants were trained to code the frequency of each politeness strategy in participants' responses. An overlapping 27% of the messages ($n = 92$) was independently coded by the two assistants. Each participant's positive and negative politeness scores were calculated as the sum of positive and negative politeness strategies the participant used, respectively. Overall politeness was calculated as the sum of positive and negative politeness scores. Intraclass correlation coefficients for the frequency of positive, negative, and overall politeness strategies were 0.82, 0.86, and 0.87, respectively. The remaining coding was evenly split between the two assistants.

Table 2.3   Positive politeness strategies and examples

Positive politeness strategies	Examples
Use informal address/greeting phrase	*Hi, eye*111111

Continued

Positive politeness strategies	Examples
Express agreement or approval of a message the support-seeker wrote in the posting	*I agree that your roommate is being unreasonable.*
Use in-group identity markers to convey in-group membership	*Some advice from a student intern herself: during your first week you will be asked to do things such file paper work, make copies, bring coffee, etc.*
Include the support-seeker in the discussion by using 1st person plural pronouns to refer to the writer or reader	*Well, we all have to start from the bottom and work our way up.*
Use discourse marker	*Please don't stress.*
Use joke or slang	*Your free labor is used for bitch work.*
Be optimistic; use optimistic words	*Best of luck with finding a new one if this one doesn't work out!*
Show sympathy or understanding of the support-seeker's feelings or situation	*I'm so sorry to hear that your boss yelled at you for being late.*
Acknowledge the support-seeker's competence or positive attributes	*Best of luck and remember you are strong person with many talents and skills!*
Soften negative attributions about the support-seeker	*Mistakes happen and it's disrespectful for him to treat you like.*
Give reasons for the recommended behavior (e.g., explaining why the suggested action will work) or ask for reasons for not doing something	*I believe that a compromise needs to be met because if the person has too much trouble doing the work in a different location or time then they have the right to use the space they pay for.*
Assume or assert reciprocity	*Reply back if you have any more concerns.*

Table 2.4   Negative politeness strategies and examples

Negative politeness strategies	Examples
Use formal address/greeting phrase	*Dear eye*111111

Continued

Negative politeness strategies	Examples
Be conventionally indirect by questioning the support-seeker's ability or willingness to perform an act	*Can you find a classmate that you can study with for the next exam?*
Hedge; using words to indicate that the writer is not assuming that the support-seeker will want to comply with the writer	*Maybe you should speak up and demand more challenging task or quit, and find another internship more worth of your time.*
Minimize the imposition; using words to imply a lesser imposition on the support-seeker than it seems	*Just give the internship a bit more time to see if it takes you anywhere.*
Show deference by using words to abase the support-provider or to raise the support-seeker's status	*My computer skills were not as good as yours.*
Impersonalize the situation or discussion by using general words	*When interns are treated unfairly, they should keep working hard to gain others' respects.*
Apologize or admit being impinging on the support-seeker's negative face	*I hate to say it, but you might be doing menial labor for quite some time before you get a "real" web design job, in this internship and in others.*

Manipulation check. To determine whether the manipulation of supportiveness of others' comments was successful, participants were asked to rate the supportiveness of the comment set they read. Eight bipolar items on an 11-point scale were used to measure supportiveness (e. g., "unsupportive-supportive" "negative-positive"). The eight items exhibited good internal consistency ($\alpha = 0.91$), and were averaged to form an index of supportiveness of others' comments. Planned comparisons were conducted to examine the difference in supportiveness across conditions. Consistent with the manipulation, supportive comments were rated as being more supportive than unsupportive comments within each topic ($ps < 0.001$). Problem topics had no effect on perceived supportiveness of comments.

The valence of a support-seeker's reply was also measured for manipulation check. Two bipolar items on an 11-point scale were used: "inappreciative-appreciative" and "negative-positive." As manipulated, the appreciative reply ($M = 8.18$, $SD = 2.68$) was perceived to be more appreciative than the inappreciative reply ($M = 7.43$, $SD = 2.67$), $t(211) = 2.04$, $p < 0.05$.

2.6 Results

With a sample of 357 participants, the power of the present study to detect a significant indirect effect at $\alpha = 0.05$ was 0.57 for small effects ($dr = 0.02$), and in approximation of 1.0 for moderate effects ($dr = 0.15$) and large effects ($dr = 0.40$).[4] Zero-order correlations among key variables are provided in Table 2.5.

Table 2.5 Zero-order correlations among variables

Variables	1	2	3	4	5	M	SD
1. Perceived public opinion	1.00					4.30	1.38
2. Liking	0.29*	1.00				4.24	1.11
3. Enacted action supportiveness	0.36*	0.24*	1.00			4.51	1.38
4. Intended action supportiveness	0.35*	0.29*	0.42*	1.00		4.41	1.32
5. Emotion-focused supportiveness	0.28*	0.20*	0.57*	0.17*	1.00	3.81	1.73
6. Politeness	0.30*	0.09	0.17*	−0.04	0.36*	1.87	1.72

Note: * $p < 0.01$.

All hypotheses were tested with PROCESS, a statistical analysis program which uses an ordinary least squares or logistic regression-based path analytical framework for estimating direct and indirect effects in mediation models (Hayes, 2013). The method of bootstrapping, which repeatedly samples the existing data, was employed to test the indirect effects. Bootstrapping has been recommended as the most powerful method for mediation analysis (Hayes, 2009; Hayes & Scharkow, 2013; Preacher & Hayes, 2008).

H1a and H2a posited that compared to participants who read unsupportive comments, those who read supportive comments would perceive the public opinion to be more supportive toward the support-seeker and perceive the support-seeker to be more likable, leading to production of higher emotion-focused support messages. To assess the concurrent mechanisms of perceived public opinion and liking, H1a and H1b were tested simultaneously with PROCESS. Supportiveness of others' comments was entered as the independent variable, perceived public opinion and liking as two parallel mediators, and emotion-focused supportiveness as the dependent variable. Problem topic was included in the research design for the purpose of enhancing generalizability of findings. It was treated as a covariate in all the hypothesis-testing analyses. A significant direct effect of supportiveness of others' comments on emotion-focused supportiveness was found, $c' = 0.82$, $t = 3.19$, $p < 0.01$. In addition, participants who read supportive comments (as opposed to unsupportive comments) perceived the public opinion to be more supportive toward the support-seeker ($a = 2.04$, $t = 19.92$, $p < 0.001$). However, readers who perceived the public opinion to be more supportive did not generate responses with higher emotion-focused supportiveness ($b = 0.10$, $t = 1.03$, $p = 0.30$). A bias-corrected bootstrap confidence interval for the indirect effect ($ab = 0.20$) based on 5,000 bootstrap samples included zero (-0.2063–0.5802). Therefore, the indirect effect of perceived public opinion was not significant. Therefore, H1a was not supported.

Compared to participants who read unsupportive comments, those who read supportive comments liked the support-seeker more ($a = 0.42$, $t = 3.49$, $p < 0.001$). Liking of the support-seeker was positively associated with emotion-focused supportiveness of readers' responses ($b = 0.20$, $t = 2.41$, $p<0.05$). Bootstrapping confirmed the mediating role of liking ($ab = 0.08$; 95% CI $= 0.0126$–0.1942). Therefore, H2a was supported.

H1b and H2b were tested with action-focused supportiveness as the dependent variable. Enacted action supportiveness was first entered as the dependent variable. The direct effect of supportiveness of others' comments on enacted action supportiveness was significant, $c' = 0.66$, $SE = 0.190$, $t = 3.41$, $p<0.001$. The supportiveness of others' comments was positively associated with perceived supportiveness of public opinion ($a = 2.04$, $t = 19.92$, $p<0.001$), and higher perceived supportiveness of public opinion led to higher supportiveness of enacted behavior in participants' responses ($b = 0.15$, $t = 2.07$, $p < 0.05$). However, the mediating effect of perceived public opinion was not confirmed by bootstrapping ($ab = 0.30$, 95% CI $= -0.0042$–0.6129). Nevertheless, liking was found to mediate the relationship between supportiveness of others' comments and supportiveness of enacted behavior in a reader's response ($a = 0.42$, $t = 3.49$, $p<0.001$; $b = 0.21$, $t = 3.40$, $p<0.001$; $ab = .09$, 95% CI $= 0.0284$–0.1831).

Intended action supportiveness was then entered separately into the model as the dependent variable. A significant direct effect of supportiveness of others' comments on the intended action supportiveness was found ($c' = 0.45$, $t = 2.39$, $p<0.05$). The indirect effect of public opinion ($a = 2.04$, $t = 19.92$, $p<0.001$; $b = 0.16$, $t = 2.25$, $p<0.05$; $ab = 0.32$, 95% CI $= 0.0540$–0.5881) and liking ($a = 0.42$, $t = 3.49$, $p<0.001$; $b = 0.25$, $t = 4.14$, $p < 0.001$; $ab = 0.10$, 95% CI $= 0.0403$–0.1924) was both significant. Therefore, H1b was partially supported and H2b was fully supported.

To test H1c and H2c, politeness (calculated as the sum of positive and negative politeness strategies used by each participant) was entered into the model as the dependent variable. The results revealed that the direct effect (c' = 0.02, t = 0.60, p = 0.55) and indirect effect of liking were insignificant (a = 0.42, t = 3.49, p<0.001; b = -0.0007, t = -0.05, p = 0.96; ab = -0.0003, 95% CI = -0.0098–0.0112). However, the indirect effect of public opinion was signficant (a = 2.04, t = 19.92, p<0.001; b = 0.05, t = 3.46, p<0.001; ab = 0.10, 95% CI = 0.0451–0.16204). This finding suggests that the perceived supportiveness in public opinion, but not liking of the support-seeker, mediated the effect of others' comments on politeness in readers' responses. Thus, H1c was supported but not H2c.

The research question aimed to assess how a support-seeker's reply to others' comments might influence readers' liking of the person, as well as the quality of support messages. A univariate analysis suggested significant difference in liking across conditions of support-seeker's reply, $F(2, 348)$ = 3.20, p<0.05, η^2 = 0.02. Post-hoc comparison using the Bonferroni test indicated that appreciative reply (M = 4.40, SD = 0.10) led to more liking of the support-seeker than inappreciative reply (M = 4.05, SD = 0.09), p<0.05. The no reply condition (M = 4.26, SD = 0.11) did not differ significantly from the appreciative or inappreciative reply condition. However, support-seeker's reply did not have an impact on any of the three features of support messages, $ps \geqslant 0.19$.

2.7 Discussion

Online support forums are relatively anonymous, less bounded by space and time, and easily accessible (Wright & Bell, 2003). These compelling advantages have made support forums a popular place to seek social support. However, the responses a support-seeker receives can vary substantially in quality, ranging from harsh condemnation to warm comfort (Aakhus & Rumsey, 2010). Not only can these responses affect a support-seeker's emotion and coping (Wright, 2000), their publicity can influence subsequent readers' perceptions and responses to the support-seeker. This study explored this phenomenon by examining how others' comments can drive people to provide more or less supportive messages to unknown others in the virtual world.

As a unique feature of participatory websites, others' comments have been studied in a variety of online contexts (Antheunis & Schouten, 2011; Lee, 2012; Walther et al. , 2008). Nevertheless, these studies focused exclusively on readers' perceptions rather than messages as outcome variables. The importance of perception resides in its guidance of message production. Without studying messages, the gap between perceptions and behaviors cannot be bridged. To the best of our knowledge, the current study was the first to look at message production under the influence of others' comments. By studying both readers' perceptions and provision of support messages online, researchers are able to empirically assess the link between perceptions and behaviors on participatory websites.

Readers' perceptions have been studied as outcomes of others' comments by communication scholars with one of two distinctive approaches (Lee & Jang, 2010; Walther et al. 2008). Literature on political communication tends to focus on the mechanism of public opinion (Lee & Jang, 2010) whereas research on interpersonal communication predominantly examines impression formation through attributions (Walther et al. , 2008, 2009). The two processes are expected to take place concurrently to influence the production of support messages. The findings largely supported this proposition by demonstrating the mediating roles of both perceived public opinion and personal liking in the link between others' comments and provision of online support messages. More specifically, the first mechanism addresses the phenomenon at a macro level by suggesting that the supportiveness of others' comments influences readers' perceptions of public opinion toward the support-seeker with regard to the focal issue, which in turn affect the quality of support messages. The other mechanism takes a micro perspective by focusing on the personal appraisal of a target. This study found that others' comments exerted influence on production of support messages through their impact on readers' liking of a support-seeker. A juxtaposition of the two mechanisms resonates with the notion of masspersonal phenomenon on these participatory websites. The visibility of the comments to other readers makes support exchange a conjunction of mass and interpersonal communication on support forums. Seen in this light, acknowledging the distinction and concurrence of both mechanisms can help us better understand and explain the communication process in online support provision and reception.

Although the findings about the influence of perceived public opinion are consistent with those documented in the conformity literature (Cialdini & Goldstein, 2004), the mechanisms underlying the influence may be different. In conformity research, appraisal of public opinion is often assumed to be driven by the desire to seek social approval and acceptance. In the current study, however, it was postulated that perceived public opinion served as a heuristic cue for making a judgment about the correct position to hold (Fein et al. , 2007; Festinger, 1950). Although these two mechanisms (i. e. , seeking social approval vs. forming accurate interpretation of reality) are arguably distinct at the theoretical level, data from this study did not allow us to empirically ascertain which mechanism was at work in online supportive communication among strangers. We thus cannot rule out the possibility that in the virtual world such as on online support forums, readers may conform to the majority view as a way to seek social approval by anonymous others. These speculations await further investigation in future research.

While functioning simultaneously, the two mechanisms were also found to exert influence of different magnitudes on the relationship between others' comments and the three features of support messages. Perceived public opinion had a stronger mediating effect on the link between others' comments and politeness; whereas liking played a major role in mediating the relationship between others' comments and emotion-focused/action-focused supportiveness. On the one hand, one possible explanation of these findings is that people rely more on external reference (e. g. , perceived public opinion) as guidance of politeness usage. On the other hand, people may use a more internal reaction (e. g. , liking) to guide their emotional and behavioral supportiveness toward a target.

Although this study focuses on online supportive communication among strangers, it has implications for the study of computer-mediated supportive communication among people who have offline relationships (Wright et al. , 2013). In supportive communication that occurs on Facebook, for example, a reader of a Facebook friend's support-seeking post is likely to know other commenters and may even have a close relationship with them. In this case, others' comments may have a stronger impact on a reader's response to a support-seeking post than they would on general online forums. In addition, it is also possible that a reader who knows the support-seeker well might be able to produce a response without much influence from others' comments. A direction for future research is to assess the role of others' comments in supportive communication on social networking sites.

Departing from a sociological or psychological approach to study social support that emphasizes the quantity of received support (i. e. , "more is better") (MacGeorge, Feng, Burleson, 2011) and following the tradition of social support research in the communication field, this study highlights the importance of "quality" in supportive communication. In particular, this study identified three conceptually related but distinctive features of person-centered support messages: emotion-focused supportiveness, action-focused supportiveness, and politeness.

Person-centeredness in supportive communication has traditionally been operationalized by measuring emotional supportiveness (MacGeorge, Feng, Burleson, 2011), which cannot represent the multifaceted nature of person-centeredness suggested in its original definition (Burleson, 1987). Although prior research evidenced the importance of behavioral supportiveness (Feng & MacGeorge, 2010), it did not theoretically incorporate this dimension into the construct of person-centeredness. Besides action-focused supportiveness, politeness was proposed as another aspect of person-centeredness in support messages. Although past research has consistently shown that attending to a support-seeker's face needs through the use of politeness strategies was an important feature of good quality support messages (Aakhus & Rumsey, 2010; Goldsmith, 1992), the current study was the first to empirically examine politeness within the framework of person-centeredness.

It should be recognized that the three dimensions of person-centeredness are distinctive but not mutually exclusive. For example, when a support-provider endorses the recipient's enacted or intended behaviors, he/she is also likely to acknowledge the recipient's feelings that arise from those behaviors. Similarly, when a support-provider approves the recipient's feelings or actions, he/she is more likely to recognize the recipient's positive attributes as well as concern for autonomy (Goldsmith, 1992). The data largely supported these propositions, showing that the three dimensions weakly to moderately correlated with each other.

One caveat concerning application of the three dimensions of person-centeredness should be noted. Although the dimensions of emotion-focused supportiveness and politeness are applicable to most situations of support provision, action-focused supportiveness may not be relevant in certain situations. For example, an individual may experience stress as a result of an event that is unrelated to his/her own behaviors (e.g., the death of a close friend). It is also likely that a support-seeker does not indicate any intention to perform certain behavior. In addition, it is worth noting that only a small number of messages exhibited very high (levels 7–9) emotion-focused supportiveness or action-focused supportiveness in this study. The theory of constructivism suggests that the production of highly person-centered messages requires both sophisticated social perception capacities and motivation (Burleson, 1987). The low frequency of highly emotion-focused and action-focused supportive messages observed in this study suggests that the participants might lack capacity or motivation, or both, to produce highly person-centered support messages to an unknown online support-seeker. Meanwhile, past research indicated that elements of highly person-centered messages might spread across many turns of supportive conversation (Jones & Wirtz, 2006), and the design of this study prevented us from observing such instances with the current data.

Besides investigating the impact of others' comments on readers' reply, this study explored how a support-seeker's reply may influence quality of support messages. Consistent with previous research (Matzat & Snijders, 2012), findings of this study suggest that a support-seeker's appreciative (versus inappreciative) reply to previous comments contributed to higher likability of the person, regardless of the valence in others' comments. The absence of a reply did not make a support-seeker more or less likable in comparison to the other two conditions. A possible explanation is that readers were fully aware of the asynchronous feature of support forums and did not expect support-seekers to reply in a timely manner. Surprisingly, valence in support-seeker's reply did not have an impact on any features of readers' support messages. One possible explanation for this finding is that the manipulation of appreciativeness in support-seeker's reply was not strong enough to produce big variation in perceptions of the appreciative and the inappreciative replies. The inappreciative reply, in particular, was perceived by participants to be more neutral than negative in appreciativeness. Future research should continue to investigate the potential influence of support-seeker's reply on readers' support provision by designing a set of replies with more salient discrepancies in valence.

Several limitations in the current study are worth discussion. First, others' comments were manipulated to be exclusively supportive or unsupportive, which imposed threat to ecological validity. In reality, although a dominant viewpoint often emerges on a topic, it is relatively uncommon to observe all comments unanimously arguing for one side. A mixture of both supportive and unsupportive messages with a discernable pattern of public opinion might increase the realism of the experiment. This study choose comments that are exclusively supportive or unsupportive to rule out the influence of possible confounding factors such as order effects of comments with different valence. Another limitation pertains to the experimental procedure. In order to examine the qualities of support messages, every participant in this study was required to reply to the support-seeker. Given that many forum users are lurkers who do not post any response after reading a post, it would be interesting to investigate whether or not participants would respond without being instructed to do so. Finally, studying initial interaction on a support forum may limit the generalizability of these findings to forum users who have prior interactions and have already developed an interpersonal relationship with other users (Tichon & Shapiro, 2003). Forum users who know a support-seeker at an interpersonal level may be less influenced by others' comments. In this case, the impact of others' comments on message quality may be attenuated. Future research can continue this line of research by studying forum users with an interaction history.

In conclusion, this study examined whether and through which mechanisms the supportiveness of others' comments to an online support-seeker's post would influence subsequent readers' responses to the support-seeker. The findings suggest that, supportive comments (as opposed to unsupportive comments) left by others not only lead subsequent readers to believe the general public would be more supportive toward the support-seeker, but also make the readers like the support-seeker more. As a result, these readers tend to provide more sensitive and polite support messages that exhibit understanding and endorsement of the support-seeker's emotions and behaviors.

Notes

1. A version of this chapter has been published as: Li, S. , Feng, B. (2015). What to say to an online support-seeker? The influence of others' responses and support-seekers' replies. *Human Communication Research*, 41, 303-326.

2. One student didn't answer the question about nationality.

3. "Student. com" is a resource website for college students, high school students, and teens. It has over 1,080,000 members and has an open forum "forums. student. com" for discussion on various topics.

4. In the survey, each participant was first required to enter the username they created on the support forum, which allows the researchers to match each participant's submitted forum response with their corresponding survey data.

References

Aakhus, M. , and Rumsey, E. (2010). Crafting supportive communication online: A communication design analysis of conflict in an online support group. *Journal of Applied Communication Research*, 38, 65-84. doi: 10.1080/00909880903483581.

Antheunis, M. L. , and Schouten, A. P. (2011). The effects of other-generated and system-generated cues on adolescents' perceived attractiveness on social setwork sites. *Journal of Computer-Mediated Communication*, 16, 391-406. doi: 10.1111/j.1083-6101.2011.01545.x.

Barak, A. , Boniel-Nissim, M. , and Suler, J. (2008). Fostering empowerment in online support groups. *Computers in Human Behavior*, 24, 1867-1883. doi: http://dx.doi.org/10.1016/j.chb.2008.02.004.

Blank, T. O. , Schmidt, S. D. , Vangsness, S. A. , Monteiro, A. K. , and Santagata, P. V. (2010). Differences among breast and prostate cancer online support groups. *Computers in Human Behavior*, 26, 1400-1404.

Brown, P., and Levinson, S. C. (1987). *Politeness: Some Universals in Language Usage*. Cambridge, UK: Cambridge University Press.

Brunswik, E. (1956). *Perception and the representative design of psychological experiments*. Berkeley: University of California Press.

Burleson, B. R. (1982). The development of comforting communication skills in childhood and adolescence. *Child Development*, 53, 1578-1588. doi: 10.1111/1467-8624.ep8588469.

Burleson, B. R. (1987). Cognitive complexity. In: J. C. McCroskey, and J. A. Daly, eds., *Personality and Interpersonal Communication*. Thousand Oaks, CA: Sage, pp. 305-349.

Burleson, B. R. (2003). Emotional support skills. In: J. O. Greene, and B. R. Burleson, eds., *Handbook of Communication and Social Interaction Skills*. Mahwah, NJ: Erlbaum, pp. 551-594.

Burleson, B. R., and Goldsmith, D. J. (1998). How the comforting process works: Alleviating emotional distress through conversationally induced reappraisals. In: P. A. Andersen, and L. K. Guerrero, eds., *Communication and Emotion*. Orlando, FL: Academic Press, pp. 246-275.

Collins, N. L., and Miller, L. C. (1994). Self-disclosure and liking: A meta-analytic review. *Psychological Bulletin*, 116, 457-475.

Coulson, N. S., Buchanan, H., and Aubeeluck, A. (2007). Social support in cyberspace: A content analysis of communication within a Huntington's disease online support group. *Patient Education and Counseling*, 68, 173-178.

Cialdini, R. B., and Goldstein, N. J. (2004). Social influence: Compliance and conformity. *Annual Review of Psychology*, 55, 591-621.

Cupach, W. R., and Carson, C. L. (2002). Characteristics and consequences of interpersonal complaints assoicated with perceived face threat. *Journal of Social and Personal Relationships*, 19, 443-462.

Edwards, C., and Edwards, A. (2013). Computer-mediated word-of-mouth communication: The influence of mixed reviews on student perceptions of instructors and courses. *Communication Education*, 62, 412-424.

Edwards, C., Edwards, A., Qing, Q., and Wahl, S. T. (2007). The influence of computer-mediated word-of-mouth communication on student perceptions of instructors and attitudes toward learning course content. *Communication Education*, 53, 255-277.

Fein, S., Goethals, G. R., and Kugler, M. B. (2007). Social influence on political judgments: The case of presidential debates. *Political Psychology*, 28, 165-192. doi: 10.2307/20447032.

Feng, B., and Burleson, B. R. (2006). Exploring the support-seeking process across cultures: Toward an integrated analysis of similarities and differences. In: M. P. Orbe, B. J. Allen and L. A. Flores, eds., *International and Intercultural Communication Annual*, 28. Thousand Oaks, CA: Sage, pp. 243-266.

Feng, B., Li, S., and Li, N. (2016). Is a profile worth a thousand words?: How online support-seeker's profile features may influence the quality of received support messages. *Communication Research*, 43(2), 253-276. doi: 10.1177/0093650213510942.

Feng, B., and MacGeorge, E. L. (2010). The influences of message and source factors on advice outcomes. *Communication Research*, 37, 553-575. doi: 10.1177/0093650210368258.

Festinger, L. (1950). Informal social communication. *Psychological Review*, 57, 271-282.

Fullwood, C., and Wootton, N. (2009). Comforting communication in an online epilepsy forum. *Journal of CyberTherapy and Rehabilitation*, 2, 159-164.

Goei, R., Lindsey, L. M., Boster, F. J., Skalski, P. D., and Bowman, J. M. (2003). The mediating roles of liking and obligation on the relationship between favors and compliance. *Communication Research*, 30, 178-197.

Goffman, E. (2003). On face-work: An analysis of ritual elements in social interaction. *Reflections*, 4, 7-13.

Goldsmith, D. J. (1992). Managing conflicting goals in supportive interaction—An intergrative theoretical framework. *Communication Research*, 19, 264-286. doi: 10.1177/009365092019002007.

Goldsmith, D. J. (1994). The role of facework in supportive communication. In: B. R. Burleson, T. L. Albrecht, and I. G. Sarason, eds., *Communication of Social Support: Messages, Interactions, Relationships, and Community*. Thousand Oaks, CA: Sage, pp. 29-49.

Goldsmith, D. J., and MacGeorge, E. L. (2000). The impact of politeness and relationship on perceived quality of advice about a problem. *Human Communication Research*, 26, 234-263. doi: 10.1111/j.1468-2958.2000.tb00757.x.

Gosling, S. D., Ko, S. J., Mannarelli, T., and Morris, M. E. (2002). A room with a cue: Personality judgments based on offices and bedrooms. *Journal of Personality and Social Psycholog*, 82, 379-398.

Hayes, A. F. (2009). Beyond Baron and Kenny: Statistical mediation analysis in the new millennium. *Communication Monographs*, 76, 408-420.

Hayes, A. F. (2013). *An introduction to mediation, moderation, and conditional process analysis: A regression-based approach*. New York: Guilford. Available from http://www.guilford.com/.

Hayes, A. F., and Scharkow, M. (2013). The relative trustworthiness of inferential tests of the indirect effect in statistical mediation analysis: Does method really matter? *Psychological Science*, 24, 1918-1927.

High, A. C., and Dillard, J. P. (2012). A review and meta-analysis of person-centered messages and social support outcomes. *Communication Studies*, 63, 99-118. doi: 10.1080/10510974.2011.598208

Jones, S. M., and Burleson, B. R. (1996). Emotion-focused and problem-focused coding system. Unpublished manuscript.

Jones, S. M., and Wirtz, J. G. (2006). How does the comforting process work?: An empirical test of an appraisal-based model of comforting.

Human Communication Research, 32, 217-243.

Kamins, M. L., and Dweck, C. S. (1999). Person versus process praise and criticism: Implications for contingent self-worth and coping. *Developmental Psychology*, 35, 835-847.

Lee, E. J. (2012). That's not the way it is: How user-generated comments on the news affect perceived media bias. *Journal of Computer-Mediated Communication*, 18, 32-45. doi: 10.1111/j.1083-6101.2012.01597.x.

Lee, E. J., and Jang, Y. J. (2010). What do others' reactions to news on Internet portal sites tell us?: Effects of presentation format and readers' need for cognition on reality perception. *Communication Research*, 37, 825-846. doi: 10.1177/0093650210376189.

Lott, A. J., and Lott, B. E. (1965). Group cohesiveness as interpersonal attraction: A review of relationships with antecedent and consequent variables. *Psychological Bulletin*, 64, 259-309.

MacGeorge, E. L. (2001). Support providers' interaction goals: The influence of attributions and emotions. *Communication Monographs*, 68, 72-97. doi: 10.1080/03637750128050.

MacGeorge, E. L., Feng, B., Butler, G. L., and Budarz, S. K. (2004). Understanding advice in supportive interactions. *Human Communication Research*, 30, 42-70. doi: 10.1111/j.1468-2958.2004.tb00724.x.

MacGeorge, E. L., Feng, B., and Burleson, B. R. (2011). Supportive communication. In: M. L. Knapp, and J. A. Daly, eds., *Handbook of Interpersonal Communication*. Thousand Oaks, CA: Sage, pp. 317-354.

MacGeorge, E. L., Feng, B., and Thompson, E. R. (2008). "Good" and "bad" advice: How to advise more effectively. In: M. T. Motley, ed., *Studies in Applied Interpersonal Communication*. Thousand Oaks, CA: Sage, pp. 145-164.

Matzat, U., and Snijders, C. (2012). Rebuilding trust in online shops on consumer review sites: Sellers' responses to user-generated complaints. *Journal of Computer-Mediated Communication*, 18, 62-79. doi: 10.1111/j.1083-6101.2012.01594.x.

Metzger, M. J., Flanagin, A. J., and Medders, R. B. (2010). Social and heuristic approaches to credibility evaluation online. *Journal of Communication*, 60, 413-439.

Preacher, K. J., and Hayes, A. F. (2008). Asymptotic and resampling strategies for assessing and comparing indirect effects in multiple mediator models. *Behavior Research Methods*, 40, 879-891.

Rains, S. A., and Young, V. (2009). A meta-analysis of research on formal computer-mediated support groups: Examining group characteristics and health outcomes. *Human Communication Research*, 35, 309-336. doi: 10.1111/j.1468-2958.2009.01353.x.

Rubin, Z. (1970). Measurement of romantic love. *Journal of Personality and Social Psychology*, 16, 265-273.

Schultz, T. (2000). Mass media and the concept of interactivity: An exploratory study of online forums and reader email. *Media, Culture, Society*, 22, 205-221.

Sherif, M., and Hovland, C. I. (1961). *Social Judgment*. New Haven, CT: Yale University Press.

Shoemaker, P. J., Breen, M., and Stamper, M. (2000). Fear of social isolation: Testing an assumption from the spiral of silence. *Irish Communications Review*, 8, 65-78.

Tanis, M. (2008). Health-related on-line forums: What's the big attraction? *Journal of Health Communication*, 13, 698-714. doi: 10.1080/108107 30802415316.

Tichon, J. G., and Shapiro, M. (2003). The process of sharing social support in cyberspace. *Cyberpsychology & Behavior*, 6, 161-170. doi: 10.1089/109493103321640356.

Uchino, B. N. (2004). *Social support and physical health: Understanding the health consequences of our relationships*. New Haven, CT: Yale University Press.

Wagoner, R., and Waldron, V. R. (1999). How supervisors convey routine bad news: Facework at UPS. *Southern Communication*

Journal, 64, 193-209.

Walther, J. B., and Boyd, S. (2002). Attraction to computer-mediated social support. In: C. A. Lin, and D. Atkin, eds., *Communication Technology and Society: Audience Adoption and Uses*. Cresskill, NJ: Hampton Press, pp. 153-188.

Walther, J. B., and Bunz, U. (2005). The rules of virtual groups: Trust, liking, and performance in computer-mediated communication. *Journal of Communication*, 55, 828-846.

Walther, J. B., Van Der Heide, B., Kim, S.-Y., Westerman, D., and Tong, S. T. (2008). The role of friends' appearance and behavior on evaluations of individuals on Facebook: Are we known by the company we keep? *Human Communication Research*, 34, 28-49. doi: 10.1111/j.1468-2958.2007.00312.x.

Walther, J. B., Van Der Heide, B., Hamel, L. M., and Shulman, H. C. (2009). Self-generated versus other-generated statements and impressions in computer-mediated communication: A test of warranting theory using Facebook. *Communication Research*, 36, 229-253.

White, M., and Dorman, S. M. (2001). Receiving social support online: Implications for health education. *Health Education Research*, 16, 693-707. doi: 10.1093/her/16.6.693.

Wright, K. (2000). Perceptions of on-line support providers: An examination of perceived homophily, source credibility, communication and social support within on-line support groups. *Communication Quarterly*, 48(1), 44-59. doi: 10.1080/01463370009385579.

Wright, K. B., and Bell, S. B. (2003). Health-related support groups on the Internet: Linking empirical findings to social support and computer-mediated communication theory. *Journal of Health Psychology*, 8, 39-54. doi: 10.1177/1359105303008001429.

Wright, K. B., Rosenberg, J., Egbert, N., Ploeger, N. A., Bernard, D. R., and King, S. (2013). Communicaiton competence, social support, and depression among college students: A model of Facebook and face-to-face support network inluence. *Journal of Health Communication*, 18, 41-57.

Xie, B. (2008). Multimodal computer-mediated communication and social support among older Chinese Internet users. *Journal of Computer-Mediated Communication*, 13, 728-750.

Yaniv, I. (2004). Receiving other people's advice: Influence and benefit. *Organizational Behavior and Human Decision Processes*, 93, 1-13. doi: http://dx.doi.org/10.1016/j.obhdp.2003.08.002.

Chapter 3　Revisiting the Impact of Others' Comments and Support-Seeker's Response on Support Provision in Online Forums

Online supportive communication has evolved into a mass social phenomenon (Barak, Boniel-Nissim, Suler, 2008). As a masspersonal medium, online support forums provide people with an innovative platform for support exchange. At the same time, interactions among support-seekers and support-providers are visible to viewers who come across the posts. Not only do comments on a given post affect viewers' perceptions of and responses to a support-seeker, whether and how the support-seeker interacts with commenters may also exert an influence on viewers' support provision.

The previous study in Chapter 2 (study 1) primarily looked at the impact of others' comments on viewers' support provision. The findings revealed that viewers exposed to supportive comments on a support-seeking post, in comparison with unsupportive comments, tended to (a) perceive the support-seeker as more likeable, (b) consider the public opinion of the support-seeker as more supportive, and thereby (c) provide more supportive responses to the support-seeker.

Several limitations with the previous study merit attention. First, it was unclear why perceived public opinion would influence viewers' responses to a support-seeking post. One possible mechanism is that people are motivated to hold accurate opinions and they believe that the majority usually represents the correct opinion. Alternatively, viewers may desire to seek approval and thus conform to public opinion in their responses, without necessarily taking into consideration the accuracy of public opinion. Study 1 was unable to emprically assess which motivation (or both) was at play.

A second limitation with study 1 concerned the manipulation of the support-seeker's reply. Study 1 revealed a positive impact of appreciative reply (versus unappreciative reply) on a support-seeker's likeability, but failed to detect its impact on supportiveness of viewers' responses. This finding might be attributed to a subtle difference between appreciative and inappreciative replies. Inappreciative reply was perceived by participants to be relatively neutral on appreciativeness. Study 2 attempted to address this limitation by improving the manipulation of appreciativeness in a support-seeker's reply. An unappreciative reply was included to directly disparage the input from previous commenters. In addition, the present study extended study 1 by examining the impact of another feature of support-seeker's reply—additional reasoning on viewers' responses to a support-seeker.

In the following sections, the rationale to explain why and how others' comments and a support-seeker's reply may affect subsequent viewers' responses to a support-seeker will be firtly laid out, and then an empirical study to test these hypotheses will be presented.

3.1 Others' Comments and Support Message

Study 1 postulated that viewers' reactions to a support-seeker would be affected by their perceptions of public opinion (Fein, Goethals, Kugler, 2007). As predicted, previous comments on a support-seeking post could affect the extent to which viewers like the support-seeker and respond supportively. To replicate this finding, a similar hypothesis is proposed.

H1: Compared to viewers exposed to unsupportive comments on a support-seeker's post, viewers exposed to supportive comments will perceive the public opinion to be more supportive of the support-seeker and will in turn provide responses with higher level of emotion-focused supportiveness and higher level of action-focused supportiveness.

However, it was unclear in study 1 why perceived public opinion affects viewers' responses to a support-seeker. Literature on conformity research has identified at least two motivations that can provide possible explanations. One is *informational conformity* motivation which is grounded in the desire to form accurate interpretations and judgments on reality. The other is *normative conformity* motivation which is primarily based on the need of gaining social approval from others (Cialdini & Goldstein, 2004; Deutsh & Gerad, 1955; Kaplan & Miller, 1987). On support forums, both informative and normative motivations may play an important role. On one hand, viewers may rely on previous comments to infer the predominant opinion, which may be considered as the most appropriate position to hold towards the support-seeker and thus influence viewers' motivation to provide more or less supportive responses. On the other hand, viewers may have a strong desire to identify with and seek approval from other members of an online community. Therefore, they may conform to the perceived consensus in their responses. Accordingly, two hypotheses are proposed based on the two motivations.

H2: The impact of others' comments on viewers' emotion-and action-focused supportiveness through perceived public opinion will be stronger for people with higher informational conformity motivation.

H3: The impact of others' comments on viewers' emotion-and action-focused supportiveness through perceived public opinion will be stronger for people with higher normative conformity motivation.

Besides perceived public opinion, previous comments may also affect viewers' impression of a support-seeker. In particular, the supportiveness of others' comments may influence subsequent readers' perceptions of the support-seeker's likeability and responses. Empirical data from study 1 support the mediating role of liking on the relationship between others' comments and supportiveness of viewers' responses. To replicate this finding, the following hypothesis is proposed.

H4: Compared to viewers exposed to unsupportive comments on a support-seeker's post, those exposed to supportive comments will perceive the support-seeker to be more likeable and will in turn provide responses with higher level of emotion-focused supportiveness and higher level of action-focused supportiveness (Figure 3.1).

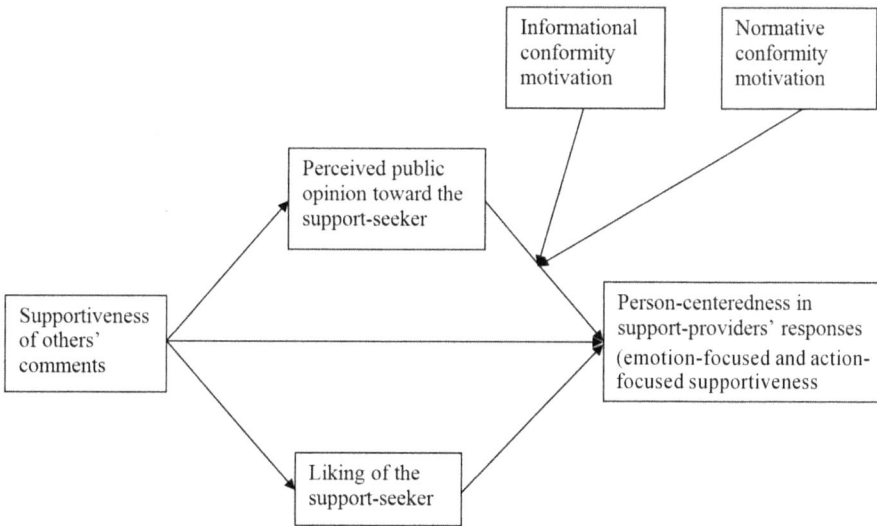

Figure 3.1   Masspersonal model of support provision online with
two motivation moderators

3.2 Appreciation Expression in Support-Seeker's Reply

In addition to support-providers' comments, support-seeker's responses to previous comments may play an important role in the supportive exchange on online support forums. Whether or not a support-seeker expresses appreciation to previous comments may influence subsequent viewers' perceptions of and responses to the support-seeker.

Most forum users are unknown to each other in their offline world and are not obliged to help others. Unlike face-to-face communication which typically contains abundant verbal and nonverbal cues, communication on online support forums represents a mediated communication that allows viewers to remain mute after reading support-seeking posts. In addition, a vast majority of support-seekers do not designate particular helper(s) in their posts, allowing viewers to lurk without any pressure. Given the minimal responsibility of viewers to respond to a support-seeking post, offering any feedback to the support-seeker can be considered a voluntary contribution.

To acknowledge voluntary commenters, support-seekers may express appreciation in their replies. However, support-seekers may respond unappreciatively or remain silent, especially after they have received undesirable comments. Whether or not a support-seeker expresses appreciation (unappreciation) to previous commenters may affect how subsequent viewers perceive the support-seeker. Research on gratitude suggests that people evaluate grateful individuals more favorably than ungrateful ones (McCullough et al. , 2001; Stein, 1989). Expression of gratitude indicates that a beneficiary values and appreciates others' assistance (Grant & Gino, 2010), making the grateful beneficiary more likeable than an ungrateful counterpart.

Gratitude expression may elicit a positive impression of a beneficiary and motivate benefactors to provide further help to the individual (McCullough et al. , 2001). Previous studies have repeatedly evidenced that receiving expression of gratitude increased a benefactor's prosocial behavior towards the beneficiary or others (Deutsch & Lamberti, 1986; Grant & Gino, 2010; McCullough et al. , 2001). Although these studies focus on the prosocial behavior of a benefactor instead of a bystander, it is reasonable to extend the findings to bystanders who witness the behavior of gratitude expression. That is, after seeing a benefactor being thanked, a bystander may also be motivated to provide support to the grateful beneficiary.

In brief, an open access to support forums allows viewers to read support-seeking posts along with responses from other commenters and support-seekers. When viewers come across a support-seeker's appreciative reply to previous commenters, they may perceive the support-seeker to be a grateful person and like him/her more, which may in turn motivate them to provide high-quality support for the support-seeker. In contrast, viewing an unappreciative reply to the commenters may create a negative impression of the support-seeker and discourage other viewers to provide high-quality support (Burleson, 1987, 2003). Accordingly, the following hypothesis is proposed.

H5: Compared to viewers exposed to a support-seeker's unappreciative reply to previous comments, viewers exposed to a support-seeker's appreciative reply will perceive the support-seeker to be more likeable and will in turn provide responses with higher level of emotion-focused supportiveness and higher level of action-focused supportiveness.

Expectancy violations theory. A theoretical framework that can shed light on the process underlying viewers' perceptions and responses to online support-seeking posts is expectancy violations theory (Burgoon, 1993; Burgoon & Hale, 1988; Burgoon & Jones, 1976). Viewers on support forums should have (implicit or explicit) expectations of support-seekers' behaviors. For instance, whether and how a support-seeker reply to previous comments may deviate from viewers' expectations and have an impact on viewers' support provision. Expectancy violations theory also provides a theoretical framework for predicting and explaining the consequences of expectancy violations in interpersonal communication (Burgoon, 1993). The theory posits that individuals' expectancies of others' communication behaviors are shaped by communicator, relationship, and context characteristics. Communicator characteristics include all features of interactants such as demographics and personality traits. Relationship characteristics include relational factors such as familiarity and status differences. Context characteristics pertain to environmental constraints of communication situations. Expectancies can be either positively or negatively violated. Positive violation tends to elicit positive evaluation and responses whereas negative violation may lead to aversive appraisals and feedback.

Viewers of a support-seeking post will likely have somewhat shared expectations of a support-seeker in an online forum. Support-seekers who benefit from voluntary support-providers may naturally feel grateful (Tsang, 2006). Therefore, on one hand, showing appreciation to people who leave supportive comments may be considered a normative behavior. On the other hand, when people are faced with criticisms from outgroup members such as unknown ones on forums, they tend to defend themselves with assertiveness (Hornsey, Oppes, Svensson, 2002). Consequently, support-seekers who defend themselves and vent their dissatisfaction to unsupportive commenters may also be understandable and cause little or no violation to viewers' expectations.

However, disconfirmation between the valence of others' comments and a support-seeker's reply may induce violation of viewers' expectations, which can further affect viewers' impression of and responses to the support-seeker. Being thankful to unsupportive commenters may violate viewers' expectations in a positive way because remaining silent or defending themselves is typical responses to criticisms (Bresnahan et al., 2002). Therefore, responding appreciatively to unsupportive commenters may lead viewers to like the support-seeker more and thus provide more supportive responses. As the other form of disconfirmation, responding unappreciatively to supportive comments might be considered as an inconsiderate and rude behavior and thus negatively violates subsequent viewers' expectation of a support-seeker's behavior, causing viewers to perceive the support-seeker aversively and reply in a less supportive way. As past research showed, even for young children, negative responses to prosocial behaviors were least frequent compared to positive or no responses (Abramovitch, Corter, Pepler, 1980). Accordingly, the following hypotheses are proposed.

H6: A support-seeker who replies unappreciatively to supportive comments will negatively violate viewers' expectations of a support-seeker's reply; whereas a support-seeker who replies appreciatively to unsupportive comments will positively violate viewers' expectations.

H7: Compared to viewers exposed to a support-seeker's unappreciative reply to supportive comments, those exposed to a support-seeker's appreciative reply to unsupportive comments will perceive the support-seeker to be more likeable and will in turn provide responses with higher level of emotion-focused supportiveness and action-focused supportiveness.

Disconfirmation between others' comments and a support-seeker's reply may trigger either positive or negative violation of viewers' expectations. However, the magnitude of positive violation may be smaller than negative violation. A positive violation of responding appreciatively to unsupportive comments may deviate from viewers' expectations to a lesser degree. Research on impression management suggests that people are motivated to maintain a positive image in front of others, especially in initial interactions (Goffman, 1959). Therefore, support-seekers may use appreciative reply as a means of strategic self-presentation that may help them obtain additional support from unknown others. Further, a general expectation of initial interaction is to have a pleasant and smooth interchange (Burgoon & Le Poire, 1993). Although unsupportive comments from others may inhibit the smoothness of a conversation, a support-seeker may desire to keep the conversation going in a constructive direction by providing an appreciative reply.

The impact of the negative violation (i. e., an inappreciative reply to supportive comments) on viewers' impression of a support-seeker may be stronger than that of the positive violation (i. e., an appreciative reply to unsupportive comments). Literature on negativity effect suggests that comparable negative and positive information (defined as being equidistant from a psychological neutral point) often are not comparable in terms of the weight they have (Kellermann, 1989), as negative information tends to be weighed more heavily in impression formation than positive information. This is mainly because positive information is more normative and thus less informative of people's personalities; whereas negative information is less typical in social interactions, especially in first-time interaction and is thus more informative (Kellermann, 1984). Responding to supportive comments in an unappreciative way is a non-normative behavior to occur during initial supportive interaction. It is thus reasonable to infer that, compared to positive violation, negative violation is more atypical and weighted more in evaluation of a support-seeker's attributes. Therefore, viewers' perceptions and responses to the support-seeker will be more affected by the negative violation. Two hypotheses are proposed.

H8: A support-seeker's unappreciative reply to supportive comments will cause a greater violation of viewers' expectation than an appreciative reply to unsupportive comments.

H9: Valence of others' comments and a support-seeker's appreciativeness will interact in such a way that appreciativeness in the reply will have a stronger effect on viewers' liking of the support-seeker, as well as action-focused and emotion-focused supportiveness of their responses in the condition of supportive comments than in the condition of unsupportive comments.

3.3 Additional Reasoning in Support-Seeker's Reply

Sharing thoughts and feelings is an essential part of support exchange on forums (Fullwood & Wootton, 2009). Besides expressing appreciation, support-seekers may want to reiterate their positions or provide additional information in their responses to previous comments. Research on social support suggests that, on one hand, support-seekers are better able to reappraise situations and cope with negative emotions if they convey their thoughts and feelings through conversations with helpers (Burleson & Goldsmith, 1998; Jones & Wirtz, 2006). On the other hand, additional thoughts and reasoning provided by support-seekers may influence the quality of supportive messages. That is, potential helpers may better understand support-seekers' needs and positions after hearing additional thoughts from support-seekers, and may be able to provide support messages with higher person-centeredness. Hence, the following hypothesis is proposed.

H10: Compared to viewers exposed to support-seeker's reply containing no additional reasoning, viewers exposed to a support-seeker's reply with additional reasoning will provide responses with higher level of emotion-focused and action-focused supportiveness.

3.4 Examining Others' Comments and Support-Seeker's Response with an Experiment

3.4.1 Participants

Data were collected from students who registered in communication or psychology classes at a large west coast university in the United States. IRB approval was obtained prior to subject recruitment. Participants were recruited through a college-wide system, and were offered extra credits for their participation. A total of 842 undergraduate students were recruited for the study. 86 cases (10.21%) were dropped due to one or more of the following reasons: participants (a) did study 1; (b) did not read the manipulated response from the support-seeker through a manipulation check; (c) correctly guessed the study's purpose; (d) questioned the realism of the webpage used in the study; or (e) whose data were not successfully saved, leaving 756 cases (24.5% male, 75.5% female; age: $M = 19.60$, $SD = 2.16$) for analysis. The majority of the participants were Asian (48%, $n = 363$), Caucasian (22.9%, $n = 173$), and Latino (19.3%, $n = 146$), but the sample also included African Americans (2.6%, $n = $

20), Native American or Alaskan Native (0.3%, $n = 2$), and other ethnicity groups (6.7%, $n = 51$).[1]

3. 4. 2 Design

This study employed a 2 (others' comments: supportive vs. unsupportive) × 3 (appreciation in seeker's reply to others' comments: appreciative reply vs. unappreciative reply vs. absence of appreciation/unappreciation) × 2 (additional reasoning in a support-seeker's reply to others' comments: presence vs. absence) × 2 (problem topic: roommate conflict vs. internship) factorial design. Consistent with study 1, the interface of a real online forum called " forums. student. com " was utilized in this study, with several modifications. First, instead of using the same profile pictures for both a support-seeker and commenters, study 2 adopted different profile pictures to distinguish the support-seeker and commenters. Second, the advertisements on the website were replaced with new ones relevant to college students' life, such as ads on studying abroad.

This study used the same topics as those in study 1. The first topic was about having conflicting schedule with roommates, and the second topic pertained to an internship disappointment. To manipulate the supportiveness of others' comments on the original post, two sets of comments differing in valence were created for each topic. Each set of comments contained four responses being exclusively supportive or unsupportive. An example of positive comment was "I totally understand you. It is ENTIRELY reasonable that you should be allowed to use your desk light to do work after 10 pm. It's your room too!" A comparable negative version was "I totally understand your roommate. It is ENTIRELY reasonable that your roommate wants you to turn off the desk light to sleep after 10 pm. It's his/her room too!" Efforts were made to keep the length and reading levels of the two versions for each comment set comparable (e. g., creating negative comments by using antonyms of the positive comments).

Manipulation of appreciation in support-seeker's reply to others' comments included three conditions: appreciative reply (i. e. , "Thank you all! You have all given me great insights that I could never have otherwise."), unappreciative reply (i. e. , "Your comments didn't add anything new."), and absence of appreciation.

Reasoning in support-seeker's reply contained two conditions: presence and absence. The presence of reasoning included two versions contingent on the topics. In the roommate post, the additional reasoning in the reply was "I should have mentioned that the light I used was a small desk light, not a floor lamp. And I already dimmed it." In the internship post, the support-seeker added in the reply "I should have mentioned that I was late for work because my dog was sick and I had to take the dog to the vet." Six versions of support-seeker's reply were created based on the different combinations of appreciation and reasoning. The support-seeker's reply was always displayed beneath the fourth comment. All other visible features of the support-seeking post (e. g. , user ID, profile) were held constant across experimental conditions.

3. 4. 3 Procedure

Upon arrival at the research lab, each participant was randomly assigned to an experimental condition and escorted by a research assistant to a cubicle with a laptop. Participants created a username and responded to the support-seeker after reading the original post and subsequent comments. After clicking the button "post a reply," the participant's response appeared immediately underneath the set of manipulated comments (and support-seeker's reply, if applicable). Each participant was only able to view his or her own response, but not responses from other participants. After submitting their responses, participants were directed to the survey system "Qualtrics" to complete a survey on their perceptions and opinions regarding the issue and the support-seeker. Upon completion of the survey, participants were thanked and debriefed.

3. 4. 4 Measures

Perceived supportiveness in public opinion. Identical to study 1, six items on a 7-point scale (1 = *strongly disagree*, 7 = *strongly agree*) were used to assess perceived supportiveness in public opinion toward the support-seeker with regard to the focal issue ($M = 4.13$, $SD = 1.30$, $\alpha = 0.93$).

Perceived accuracy of public opinion. This variable was measured by six items on a 7-point Likert-scale (1 = *strongly disagree*, 7 = *strongly agree*) ("Majority beliefs often reflect accurate interpretations of reality."). Since there was no existing measure on this variable, the items were constructed based on the literature on conformity research (Cialdini & Goldstein, 2004). The scale exhibited high reliability ($M = 3.19$, $SD = 1.21$, $\alpha = 0.90$).

Need for social approval. A scale of ten items on a 7-point scale (1 = *strongly disagree*, 7 = *strongly agree*) modified from the short version of the Martin-Larsen approval motivation scale (MLAM; Martin, 1984) was used to measure viewers' need for social approval (e.g., "In order to get along and be liked, I tend to be what people expect me to be."). The reliability was satisfactory ($M = 3.64$, $SD = 0.85$, $\alpha = 0.76$).

Liking of the support-seeker. The same scale of six items on a 7-point scale (1 = *strongly disagree*, 7 = *strongly agree*) used in study 1 was employed to measure participants' liking toward the support-seeker ($M = 4.19$, $SD = 1.08$, $\alpha = 0.94$).

Expectedness of support-seeker's reply. A scale of five items on a 7-point Likert-scale (1 = *strongly disagree*, 7 = *strongly agree*) modified from scales developed by Afifi and Metts (1998) as well as Burgoon and Walther (1990) was used to measure the valence of violation caused by appreciation/unappreciation in a support-seeker's reply (e.g., "The support-seeker replied in a way that most people would find positive."). This scale exhibited high internal consistency ($M = 4.16$, $SD = 1.39$, $\alpha = 0.89$).

Another measure of five items on a 5-point scale ($1 =$ *not at all*, $5 =$ *completely*) modified from the same scales (Afifi & Metts, 1998; Burgoon & Walther, 1990) was used to assess the magnitude of violation (e. g. , "The support-seeker replied in a way I didn't expect." $M = 2.54$, $SD = 0.95$, $\alpha = 0.84$).

Coding for emotion-focused supportiveness. The nine-level hierarchy of emotion-focused supportiveness adopted in study 1 was also used in this study. Each message was coded into one of the nine sublevels embedded in the three major levels. An overlapping 22% of the messages ($n = 167$) was independently coded by two coders and reached satisfactory reliability (Krippendorff's $\alpha = 0.72$). After resolving discrepancies through discussions, the two coders evenly split the rest of data and coded them separately.

Coding for action-focused supportiveness. This study adopted the nine-level coding hierarchy of action-focused supportiveness used in study 1. The degree of supportiveness regarding the target's enacted/intended behaviors increased with the levels. Two subcategories of enacted and intended behaviors were coded separately. Two coders coded an overlapping 20% of all cases ($n = 155$). Coding agreement on supportiveness of enacted and intended actions were 0.70 and 0.78 (Krippendorff's α), respectively. The coders resolved the discrepancies through discussions and split the remaining messages to code.

Manipulation check. To determine whether the manipulation of supportiveness of others' comments was successful, participants were asked to rate the supportiveness of the comment set they read. A scale of eight items on a 7-point Likert-scale ($1 =$ *strongly disagree*, $7 =$ *strongly agree*) was used to measure supportiveness (e. g. , "Overall, I think others' comments to the original poster were supportive."). The scale manifested high internal consistency ($\alpha = 0.92$). The set of supportive comments ($M = 5.41$, $SD = 0.79$) was perceived to be significantly more supportive than the set of unsupportive comments ($M = 2.94$, $SD = 1.03$), $t(672) = 36.20$, $p < 0.001$.

Appreciativeness of support-seeker's reply was accessed with four items on a 7-point Likert-scale (1 = *strongly disagree*, 7 = *strongly agree*) (e.g. "Overall, I think the original poster's reply to others' comments was appreciative."). In the four conditions that did not include a support-seeker's reply, participants were not asked to answer these questions. The scale exhibited high reliability ($\alpha = 0.94$). Appreciative reply ($M = 6.15$, $SD = 0.84$) was evaluated as significantly more appreciative than unappreciative one ($M = 3.18$, $SD = 1.33$), $F(2, 621) = 452.36$, $p < 0.001$.

In conditions that containing a support-seeker's reply, participants were also asked three questions on a 7-point Likert-scale ($\alpha = 0.94$) to assess the amount of additional reasoning in a support-seeker's reply (e.g., "The support-seeker offers additional justification in the reply."). A support-seeker's reply that included additional reasoning ($M = 5.45$, $SD = 1.31$), was perceived to have more reasoning than a reply without additional reasoning ($M = 2.33$, $SD = 1.32$), $t(623) = 29.04$, $p < 0.001$. There was no significant difference between the two topic conditions in terms of amount of additional reasoning, $t(623) = 1.56$. $p = 0.12$.

3.5 Results

Like study 1, PROCESS was employed as the main statistical tool to analyze hypotheses involving mediation and moderation. T-test and ANOVA were also used to compare mean differences and examine interactions. Topic was entered as a covariate unless it was noted otherwise. Zero-ordered correlations among key variables are presented in Table 3.1.

Table 3.1　Zero-order correlations among variables

No.	Variables	1	2	3	4	5	6	7	8	M	SD
1.	Perceived public opinion	1.00								4.13	1.30

Continued

No.	Variables	1	2	3	4	5	6	7	8	M	SD
2.	Information conformity motivation	0.06	1.00							3.19	1.21
3.	Normative conformity motivation	0.03	0.29**	1.00						3.64	0.85
4.	Liking	0.15**	0.15**	0.04	1.00					4.19	1.08
5.	Violation valence	0.05	0.10*	0.03	0.57**	1.00				4.16	1.39
6.	Violation magnitude	−0.09*	0.04	0.11**	−0.19**	−0.35**	1.00			2.54	0.95
7.	Emotion-focused supportiveness	0.13**	−0.02	−0.06	0.20**	0.06	−0.03	1.00		4.03	1.57
8.	Enacted behavior supportiveness	0.27**	0.03	0.04	0.17**	0.02	−0.01	0.37**	1.00	4.76	0.99
9.	Intended behavior supportiveness	0.27**	0.00	0.03	0.09*	0.06	0.01	0.05	0.27**	4.55	1.27

Note: *** $p < 0.001$; ** $p < 0.01$; * $p < 0.05$.

H1 predicted that compared to viewers of unsupportive comments, viewers exposed to supportive comments would perceive the public to be more supportive of the support-seeker and thus provide responses with higher emotion-focused and action-focused supportiveness. First, emotion-focused supportiveness was entered as the dependent variable into PROCESS; supportiveness of others' comments and perceived public opinion were entered as independent variable and mediator separately. Consistent with the prediction, viewers of supportive comments would perceive the public to be more supportive ($a = 1.55$, $t = 20.36$, $p < 0.001$) and in turn provided responses with higher emotion-focused supportiveness ($b = 0.16$, $t = 3.10$, $p < 0.01$). The indirect effect was confirmed by a 5,000 resampling boostrapping test ($ab = 0.25$; 95% CI $= 0.0865–0.4144$). Perceived public opinion fully mediated the relationship between supportiveness of others' comments and emotion-focused supportiveness in viewers' responses as the direct effect was insignificant ($c' = -0.02$, $t = -0.14$, $p = 0.89$). Second, two aspects of action-focused supportiveness, enacted behavior and intended behavior, were entered as the dependent variables separately. Perceived public opinion was found to fully mediate the relationship between supportiveness of others' comments and supportiveness of enacted behavior in viewers' responses ($a = 1.55$, $t = 20.36$, $p < 0.001$; $b = 0.21$, $t = 6.35$, $p < 0.001$; $ab = 0.33$; 95% CI $= 0.2224–0.4400$; $c' = -0.02$, $t = -0.21$, $p = 0.83$). In addition, perceived public opinion partially mediated the relationship between supportiveness of others' comments and supportiveness of intended behavior in viewers' responses ($a = 1.55$, $t = 20.36$, $p < 0.001$; $b = 0.21$, $t = 5.24$, $p < 0.001$; $ab = 0.33$; 95% CI $= 0.2040–0.4579$; $c' = 0.23$, $t = 2.21$, $p < 0.05$). Therefore, H1 gained full support.

H2 posited a moderated mediation such that the mediating effect of perceived public opinion on the relationship between supportiveness of others' comments and supportiveness in viewers' responses was contingent on viewers' informational conformity motivations. Model 14 in PROCESS was used to test this hypothesis. The results revealed that people with stronger informational conformity motivation were more affected by others' comments on their emotion-focused and action-focused supportiveness through perceived public opinion (Tables 3.2–3.5). Therefore, H2 was supported.

Table 3.2   Model coefficients for moderated mediation in H2

Antecedent		M (PubOp)			Y_1 (Emotion)			Y_2 (Enacted behavior)			Y_3 (Intended behavior)	
		Coeff.	SE		Coeff.	SE		Coeff.	SE		Coeff.	SE
X (Comments)	a	1.55^{***}	0.08	c'	-0.06	0.13		-0.05	0.09		0.21	0.11
M (PubOp)				b_1	-0.07	0.11		-0.03	0.07		-0.07	0.08
V (InfoCon)				b_2	-0.37^{**}	0.14		-0.32^{***}	0.09		-0.39	0.11
$M \times V$				b_3	0.08^{*}	0.03		0.08^{***}	0.02		0.09^{***}	0.02
Constant	i_1	3.31^{***}	0.07	i_2	4.00^{***}	0.46		4.92^{***}	0.29		5.08^{***}	0.36
		$R^2 = 0.36$			$R^2 = 0.13$			$R^2 = 0.10$			$R2 = 0.18$	
		$F_{(2, 746)} =$ 207.92***			$F_{(5, 743)} =$ 22.39***			$F_{(5, 743)} =$ 15.97***			$F_{(5, 743)} =$ 31.71***	

Note: *** $p<0.001$; ** $p<0.01$; * $p<0.05$.

Table 3.3   Conditional indirect effect of comments on emotion-focused supportiveness at values of informational conformity motivation

Moderator (informational conformity motive) value	Conditional indirect effect at mean and ± 1SD			
	Boot indirect effect	Boot SE	Boot LLCI	Boot ULCI
Low, $-1SD(1.98)$	0.18	0.08	0.03	0.34
Average (3.19)	0.36	0.06	0.24	0.49
High, $+1SD(4.40)$	0.54	0.09	0.37	0.71

Note: Values for the moderator are the mean and plus/minus one SD from mean.

Table 3.4   Conditional indirect effect of comments on enacted behavior supportiveness at values of informational conformity motivation

Moderator (Informational conformity motive) value	Conditional indirect effect at mean and ± 1SD			
	Boot indirect effect	Boot SE	Boot LLCI	Boot ULCI
Low, $-1SD(1.98)$	0.20	0.07	0.05	0.34

Continued

Moderator (Informational conformity motive) value	Conditional indirect effect at mean and ± 1SD			
	Boot indirect effect	Boot SE	Boot LLCI	Boot ULCI
Average (3.19)	0.35	0.06	0.24	0.48
High, +1SD(4.40)	0.51	0.07	0.37	0.66

Note: Values for the moderator are the mean and plus/minus one SD from mean.

Table 3.5　Conditional indirect effect of comments on intended behavior supportiveness at values of informational conformity motivation

Moderator (informational conformity motive) value	Conditional indirect effect at mean and ± 1SD			
	Boot indirect effect	Boot SE	Boot LLCI	Boot ULCI
Low, -1SD(1.98)	0.18	0.08	0.03	0.35
Average (3.19)	0.36	0.06	0.24	0.49
High, +1SD(4.40)	0.54	0.08	0.38	0.71

Note: Values for the moderator are the mean and plus/minus one SD from mean.

H3 proposed a similar moderated mediation with normative conformity motivation being the moderator. No significant interaction between perceived public opinion and normative conformity motivation was found with regard to emotion and action-focused supportiveness ($ps>0.68$). This result indicates that the effects of perceived public opinion on supportiveness in viewers' responses (both emotion and action-focused supportiveness) were not contingent on the level of normative conformity motivation. Therefore, H3 was not supported.

H4 hypothesized that liking of the support-seeker would mediate the relationship between others' comments and viewers' responses. Contradictory to the prediction, viewers of unsupportive comments ($M = 4.28$, $SD = 0.05$) liked the support-seeker more than viewers of supportive comments ($M = 4.10$, $SD = 0.06$; $a = -0.18$, $t = -2.35$, $p<0.05$). Liking in turn led to higher emotion-focused supportiveness ($b = 0.26$, $t = 5.23$, $p<0.001$; $ab = -0.05$; 95% CI $= -0.0988-0.0097$; $c' = 0.29$, $t = 2.69$, $p<0.01$), enacted behavior supportiveness ($b = 0.17$, $t = 5.25$, $p < 0.001$; $ab = -0.03$; 95% CI $= -0.0687$–0.0060; $c' = 0.35$, $t = 5.02$, $p < 0.001$), as well as intended behavior supportiveness in viewers' responses ($b = 0.16$, $t = 3.96$, $p < 0.001$; $ab = -0.03$; 95% CI $= -0.0682$–0.0066; $c' = 0.59$, $t = 6.91$, $p < 0.001$). Thus, H4 was partially supported.

H5 postulated that appreciativeness in a support-seeker's reply would affect the supportiveness of viewers' responses through its impact on likeability of the support-seeker. In order to fully represent the effect of a categorical variable with k mutually exclusive categories on other variables, k-1 parameter estimates are needed (Hayes & Preacher, 2014). Mediate Macro is such a program in which dummy code is an independent variable and assesses its indirect effect (Hayes & Preacher, 2014). The first dummy variable ($D1$) coded absence of appreciativeness, the second dummy variable ($D2$) coded appreciative reply, and unappreciative reply functioned as the reference group and coded zero on both $D1$ and $D2$. Emotion-focused and action-focused supportiveness were entered as the dependent variables respectively. Results indicated that compared to viewers of unappreciative reply, viewers of appreciative reply would like the support-seeker more ($a = 0.78$, $t = 8.44$, $p < 0.001$), and thereby provided responses with higher emotion-focused ($b = 0.26$, $t = 5.07$, $p < 0.001$; $ab = 0.21$; 95% CI $= 0.1209$–0.3098; $c' = -0.13$, $t = -0.93$, $ns.$), enacted behavior ($b = 0.19$, $t = 5.45$, $p < 0.001$; $ab = 0.15$; 95% CI $= 0.0917$–0.2134; $c' = -0.26$, $t = -2.82$, $p < 0.01$), and intended behavior supportiveness ($b = 0.14$, $t = 3.13$, $p < 0.01$; $ab = 0.11$; 95% CI $= 0.0410$–0.1892; $c' = 0.005$, $t = 0.04$, $ns.$). H5 was supported.

H6 through H8 compared viewers' perceptions of and responses to a support-seeker in two conditions, unappreciative reply to supportive comments (Condition 1) and appreciative reply to unsupportive comments (Condition 2). H6 proposed that unappreciative reply to supportive comments would elicit negative violation whereas appreciative reply to unsupportive comments would trigger positive violation of viewers' expectations. Two one-sample t-tests were conducted with violation valence in each condition comparing to the mid-point 4 (neutral on violation valence) respectively. As predicted, viewers perceived unappreciative reply to supportive comments a negative violation ($M = 2.89$, $SD = 1.23$, $t(127) = -10.23$, $p<0.001$) and appreciative reply to unsupportive comments a positive violation ($M = 5.29$, $SD = 0.92$, $t(117) = 15.22$, $p<0.001$).

　　H7 predicted that relative to negative violation, viewers who experienced positive violation would like the support-seeker more and thus provided responses with higher emotion-focused and action-focused supportiveness. Due to difficulty in separating and comparing two cells in factorial design which was intertwined with a mediation analysis, only data on positive and negative violations were included in the analysis. A major concern of partialling out the rest of data in the analysis was that the power would decrease as the sample size decreased (Keppel & Wickens, 2004). In this study, however, each condition had more than enough cases ($ns>110$). Power should not be a big concern. Results suggested that compared to unappreciative reply to supportive comments, appreciative reply to unsupportive comments led to higher likeability of the support-seeker ($a = 1.10$, $t = 8.54$, $p<0.001$) and thereby more supportive responses in terms of enacted ($b = 0.14$, $t = 2.42$, $p<0.05$; $ab = 0.16$; 95% CI = $0.0247-0.3152$; $c' = -0.58$, $t = -4.20$, $p<0.001$) and intended behaviors ($b = 0.20$, $t = 2.68$, $p<0.01$; $ab = 0.22$; 95% CI = $0.0471-0.4267$; $c' = -0.75$, $t = -4.34$, $p<0.001$), but not emotion ($b = 0.17$, $t = 1.75$, $p = 0.08$; $ab = 0.18$; 95% CI = $-0.0158-0.3987$; $c' = -0.34$, $t = -1.60$, $p = 0.11$). Therefore, H7 was partially supported.

　　H8 tested the hypothesis that unappreciative reply to supportive comments would elicit greater violation than appreciative reply to unsupportive comments, regardless of violation valence. A planned comparison was conducted and revealed no significant difference between the two conditions ($M_n = 3.14$, $SD_n = 1.03$; $M_p = 3.06$, $SD_p = 0.89$), $t(614) = .71$, $p = 0.48$.

　　H9 was concerned with the interaction between other's comments and appreciativeness in a support-seeker's reply. In particular, it hypothesized that appreciativeness would have a stronger effect on a support-seeker's likeability and viewers' responses in the condition of supportive comments than in the condition of unsupportive comments. The results, however, did not support this hypothesis as none of the two-way interactions was significant ($ps > 0.07$). H9 was not supported.

H10 postulated that inclusion of additional reasoning in a support-seeker's reply would affect the quality of viewers' responses. However, no main effect was found along any of the dimensions of response supportiveness, $ps > 0.23$. H10 was not supported.

3.6 Discussion

Online support forums provide people a relatively innovative means to seek and provide social support among weak ties from a distance. Given that a potentially infinite number of people may read a support-seeking post, the opportunity of receiving support significantly increases. However, an increased amount of received support may not come with enhanced quality of support (MacGeorge, Feng, Burleson, 2011). It is thus theoretically and pragmatically important to identify factors that influence the quality of support provided on online forums. Taking a message-centered approach, the current study examined two potential factors, users' comments to a support-seeking post and the support-seeker's response to previous comments.

This study largely replicated findings in study 1 with regard to the impact of others' comments on viewers' responses through two mechanisms, one at an interpersonal level of liking, and the other at a macro level of public opinion. Consistent with study 1, others' comments affected viewers' perceptions of public opinion as well as their liking of a support-seeker, which in turn influenced supportiveness in viewers' responses. However, one unexpected finding was that viewers of unsupportive comments liked the support-seeker more than viewers of supportive comments, although the difference was relatively small. It was possible that valence of others' comments alone could not fully explain its impact on the support-seeker's likeability, especially considering the role of appreciativeness in a support-seeker's reply. Support-seekers who responded appreciatively were perceived to be more likable than those who responded unappreciatively. The interaction of others' comments and appreciativeness in a support-seeker's reply may complicate the situation. For example, compared to viewers of supportive comments yet unappreciative reply, those exposed to unsupportive comments yet appreciative reply were found to like the support-seeker more.

Regarding the macro mechanism of public opinion, one unaddressed question in study 1 was why viewers would conform to the perceived public opinion in their responses to the support-seeker. The present study tapped into this question by examining the moderating role of different conformity motivations on the relationship between perceived public opinion and viewers' responses. Extant literature has identified two distinctive motivations, namely informational and normative conformity motivations (Cialdini & Goldstein, 2004; Deutsch & Gerard, 1955). Despite their conceptual distinction, relatively little research attention has been devoted to explicating and empirically differentiating the two concepts (Cialdini & Goldstein, 2004). This study attempted to fill this gap by directly measuring the two motivations. The findings suggested that people with stronger informational conformity motivation would be more affected by perceived public opinion on their responses because they are more inclined to believe that the majority represents accurate opinions on given issues. However, normative conformity motivation did not exert a significant influence. That is, viewers who desire more social approval did not conform more to perceived public opinion in their responses than viewers with lower motivation for social approval. Rather, people are likely to adopt public opinion because they tend to believe it is the correct viewpoint. On online support forums, in particular, people may care little about getting approval from unknown anonymous others. This idea is in line with the notion of reference group (Oshagan, 1996; Scheufle & Moy, 2000), which may play a more important role than general public in affecting an individual's behavior in online communities. In other words, if previous comments were generated by reference groups such as viewers' friends, viewers who have stronger normative conformity motivation might be more affected by earlier comments on their perceptions and behaviors. For example, on social networking sites such as Facebook where commenters are identifiable and may be offline friends, viewers may have a stronger motivation to obtain approval from previous commenters and thus be more affected by their opinions. Online supportive communication among strong ties could be a fruitful avenue of future research.

Besides supportiveness of others' comments, this study continued its investigation on a support-seeker's reply. Study 1 found that an appreciative reply (compared to an unappreciative reply) increased a support-seeker's likeability yet caused no difference in viewers' responses, which may be partly due to the perceived neutrality of the inappreciative reply. Revisiting this issue with a stronger manipulation on appreciativeness, this study found that relative to an unappreciative reply, an appreciative reply made a support-seeker more likeable and elicited more supportive responses. The positive impact of appreciativeness on support provision offers practical guidance for online support-seekers. A support-seeker will ultimately benefit from expressing their gratitude to voluntary commenters because subsequent viewers will have a more positive impression of the support-seeker and thus provide more supportive responses. From a pragmatic perspective, acknowledging previous commenters with a generic remark may cost little comparing to the reward of receiving high-quality support. Future research may also examine whether having individualized response for each commenter may affect the quality of viewers' support. Considering that customizing responses takes more time and energy, a support-seeker might be perceived as more likable and receive more supportive responses from subsequent viewers.

Another topic to investigate is the ongoing interaction between a support-seeker and a designated support-provider on support forums. It will be interesting to examine whether a support-provider is more likely to provide further help with more supportiveness if a support-seeker has responded to his/her earlier comment.

Within the framework of expectancy violations theory, this study examined how valence of others' comments and appreciation in a support-seeker's reply interacts to violate viewers' expectations and affect their support provisions. Consistent with study 1, two-way interactions remained insignificant with regard to the dependent measures on viewers' responses. However, an investigation of two specific types of disconfirmation (i.e., unappreciative reply to supportive comments vs. appreciative reply to unsupportive comments) generated some interesting findings. As hypothesized, appreciative reply to unsupportive comments caused positive violations of viewers' expectations whereas unappreciative reply to supportive comments led to negative violations. In addition, viewers of the former would like the support-seeker more and reply with higher action-focused supportiveness (but not emotion-focused supportiveness) than viewers of the latter. On a variety of participatory websites, including but not limited to support forums, a primary author/owner of a webpage may sometimes encounter negative feedback from others and be inclined to argue with the commenters or stay mute. Resisting the temptation to stir up a dispute and acknowledging the commenters may potentially turn the tide by positively violating subsequent viewers' expectations, which may lead to positive feedback. Meanwhile, negative violation such as scorning others' input will often lead to unconstructive communication and should be avoided under most circumstances. Besides appreciativeness, future research may also explore other forms of feedback from support-seekers and their impact on viewers' perceptions and support provision. Studying online shopping, Matzat and Snijders (2012) found that apology was always more effective in rebuilding trust than denial when online sellers were faced with consumers' accusations.

Likewise, responses such as apology or denial could be studied in the context of online support forums.

Extending study 1, this study examined another component of support-seeker's reply-additional reasoning-providing additional information to justify their behaviors mentioned in the original post. It was predicted that viewers of a support-seeker's reply involving additional reasoning would like the support-seeker more and provide more supportive responses than viewers not exposed to additional reasoning. Findings of this study did not support this prediction. However, an exploratory analysis found evidence of an indirect effect of additional reasoning in a support-seeker's reply on viewers' responses through liking of the support-seeker. While conventional wisdom would challenge the existence of an indirect effect due to an absence of total effect, modern approaches would argue otherwise. That is, an indirect effect is likely to exist without an association between the independent and dependent variables because multiple intervening variables may mediate a relationship in opposite directions and thus cancel out the effect of each other (Hayes, 2009). Therefore, it is possible that some unknown variables mediated the relationship between additional reasoning and viewers' responses in the opposite direction to the effect of support-seeker's likeability. One possible mechanism to explain the indirect effect through liking is that additional reasoning may attenuate a support-seeker's accountability on the conflict (MacGeorge, 2001) and make subsequent viewers like the support-seeker more, leading to more supportive responses. One caveat to this finding is that additional reasoning may not always be perceived in a positive manner (Matzat & Snijders, 2012). When additional reasoning is embedded in an unappreciative reply, people may consider justifications as excuses or denials and may have decreased likeability of a support-seeker. Despite the lack of direct test of this speculation, the current data indicated that an unappreciative reply combined with additional reasoning led to less likeability of a support-seeker, compared to an appreciative reply followed by additional reasoning.

In conjunction with study 1, this project emphasized quality of support messages with an examination of both emotion-and action-focused supportiveness. Emotion-focused supportiveness represents the extent to which a message acknowledges and validates a target's feelings and emotions, as well as helps the target to reappraise the situation. Action-focused supportiveness concerns the degree to which a message endorses/ recommends a target's enacted/intended behaviors. While these two dimensions capture different aspects on message supportiveness, they may have some overlap because offering emotional support sometimes requires addressing behaviors.

Few messages in this study exhibited high levels (levels 7-9) of emotion-or action-focused supportiveness, demonstrating a similar trend found in study 1. According to constructivism, the production of high-quality support messages requires both capacity and motivation (Burleson, 1987, 1990, 2003). Participants may consider the study a task to complete for extra credit and thus be less motivated to reply with high-quality support, compared to online support forum users. High levels of supportiveness may also be more common in extended conversations which take more turns to facilitate support-seekers' reappraisals (Burleson & Goldsmith, 1998). In this study, support-seekers and -providers only responded once to each other without subsequent interactions. It is also reasonable to anticipate more messages with highly action-focused supportiveness in face-to-face communication where tangible behavioral support is more feasible.

Several limitations need to be addressed. First, in order to acquire enough responses and to analyze message features, all participants were instructed to reply to the support-seeker; whereas in reality many viewers are lurkers and never respond. It will be interesting to see how others' comments and a support-seeker's reply, along with other factors, may influence viewers' likelihood to respond in the first place. Second, compared to voluntary support forum users, the current sample of college students may be less motivated to respond, leading to a deflated quality of message supportiveness. Replicating this study with a sample of active forum users may help provide meaningful comparisons and produce more generalizable findings.

3.7 Conclusion

Supportive communication is a common component of our daily interactions. Although people often cope with these difficult times by seeking support from those in their social networks, more and more people are turning to the cyberspace for help (Rains, Peterson, Wright, 2015). This project presented two experiments in an effort to understand the interactions between online support-seekers and -providers on support forums. In general, viewers of supportive comments would perceive the public opinion to be more supportive of support-seeker and thus provide responses with higher emotion- and action-focused supportiveness. The stated effect was stronger for viewers who had more faith in public opinion. Others' comments also affect viewers' support provision through the liking of a support-seeker, with higher liking eliciting more supportive responses. As a support-seeker, expressing appreciation to voluntary commenters can enhance their likeability and chance of receiving high-quality support from subsequent viewers.

Supportive communication on online forums is a complex and dynamic process shaped and affected by a variety of factors such as senders, receivers, and contexts. It is a form of masspersonal communication because it characterizes features of both mass communication and interpersonal communication. On one hand, support-seekers and -providers may engage in interpersonal communication if they use personalized messages to address one another. On the other hand, mass communication takes place as support-seekers and -providers target a potentially large audience in their messages. Meanwhile, the interactions among support-seekers and -providers are visible to all viewers who come across the thread. An integration of mass and interpersonal communication makes supportive communication on participatory websites such as online forums a unique process to study.

Note

1. One student didn't answer the question about nationality.

References

Abramovitch, R., Corter, C., and Pepler, D. J. (1980). Observations of Mixed-Sex Sibling Dyads. *Child Development*, 51(4), 1268-1271. doi: 10.2307/1129570.

Afifi, W. A., and Metts, S. (1998). Characteristics and consequences of expectation violations in close relationships. *Journal of Social and Personal Relationships*, 15, 365-392.

Barak, A., Boniel-Nissim, M., and Suler, J. (2008). Fostering empowerment in online support groups. *Computers in Human Behavior*, 24, 1867-1883. doi: http://dx.doi.org/10.1016/j.chb.2008.02.004.

Bresnahan, M. J., Shearman, S. M., Lee, S. Y., Ohashi, R., and Mosher, D. (2002). Personal and cultural differences in responding to criticism in three countries. *Asian Journal of Social Psychology*, 5(2), 93-105. doi: 10.1111/1467-839X.00097.

Burgoon, J. K. (1993). Interpersonal expectations, expectancy violations, and emotional communication. *Journal of Language and Social Psychology*, 12, 30-48.

Burgoon, J. K., and Hale, J. L. (1988). Nonverbal expectancy violations: Model elaboration and application to immediacy behaviors. *Communication Monographs*, 55, 58-79. doi: 10.1080/03637758809376158.

Burgoon, J. K., and Jones, S. B. (1976). Toward a theory of personal space expectations and their violations. *Human Communication Research*,

2, 131-146.

Burgoon, J. K., and Le Poire, B. A. (1993). Effects of communication expectancies, actual communication, and expectancy disconfirmation on evaluations of communicators and their communication behavior. *Human Communication Research*, 20, 67-96.

Burgoon, J. K., and Walther, J. B. (1990). Nonverbal expectancies and the consequences of violations. *Human Communication Research*, 17, 232-265.

Burleson, B. R. (1987). Cognitive complexity. In: J. C. McCroskey, and J. A. Daly, eds., *Personality and Interpersonal Communication*. Thousand Oaks, CA: Sage, pp. 305-349.

Burleson, B. R. (1990). Comforting as social support: Relational consequences of supporting behaviors. In: S. Duck, ed., *Personal Relationships and Social Support*. London: Sage, pp. 66-82.

Burleson, B. R. (2003). Emotional support skills. In: J. O. Greene, and B. R. Burleson, eds., *Handbook of Communication and Social Interaction Skills*. Mahwah, NJ: Erlbaum, pp. 551-594.

Burleson, B. R., and Goldsmith, D. J. (1998). How the comforting process works: Alleviating emotional distress through conversationally induced reappraisals. In: P. A. Andersen, and L. K. Guerrero, eds., *Communication and Emotion*. Orlando, FL: Academic Press, pp. 246-275.

Cialdini, R. B., and Goldstein, N. J. (2004). Social influence: Compliance and conformity. *Annual Review of Psychology*, 55, 591-621.

Deutsch, M., and Gerard, H. B. (1955). A study of normative and informative social influences upon indiviudal judgment. *Journal of Abnormal and Social Psychology*, 51, 629-636.

Deutsch, F. M., and Lamberti, D. M. (1986). Does social approval increase helping? *Personality and Social Psychology Bulletin*, 12(2), 149-157. doi: 10.1177/0146167286122001.

Fein, S., Goethals, G. R., and Kugler, M. B. (2007). Social influence on political judgments: The case of presidential debates. *Political*

Psychology, 28, 165-192. doi: 10.2307/20447032.

Fullwood, C., and Wootton, N. (2009). Comforting communication in an online epilepsy forum. *Journal of Cyber Therapy and Rehabilitation*, 2, 159-164.

Goffman, E. (1959). *The Presentation of Self in Everyday Life*. New York: Anchor.

Grant, A. M., and Gino, F. (2010). A little thanks goes a long way: Explaining why gratitude expressions motivate prosocial behavior. *Journal of Personality and Social Psychology*, 98(6), 946-955. doi: http://dx.doi.org/10.1037/a0017935.

Hayes, A. F. (2009). Beyond Baron and Kenny: Statistical mediation analysis in the new millennium. *Communication Monographs*, 76, 408-420.

Hayes, A. F., and Preacher, K. J. (2014). Statistical mediation analysis with a multicategorical independent variable. *British Journal of Mathematical and Statistical Psychology*, 67(3), 451-470. doi: 10.1111/bmsp.12028.

Hornsey, M. J., Oppes, T., and Svensson, A. (2002). "It's OK if we say it, but you can't": Responses to intergroup and intragroup criticism. *European Journal of Social Psychology*, 32(3), 293-307. doi: 10.1002/ejsp.90.

Jones, S. M., and Wirtz, J. G. (2006). How does the comforting process work?: An empirical test of an appraisal-based model of comforting. *Human Communication Research*, 32, 217-243.

Kaplan, M. F., and Miller, C. E. (1987). Group decision making and normative versus informational influence: Effects of type of issue and assigned decision rule. *Journal of Personality and Social Psychology*, 53, 306-313.

Kellermann, K. (1984). The negativity effect and its implications for initial interaction. *Communication Monographs*, 51, 37-55.

Kellermann, K. (1989). The negativity effect in interaction: It's all in your point of view. *Human Communication Research*, 16, 147-183.

Keppel, G., and Wickens, T. D. (2004). *Design and Analysis: A Researcher's*

Handbook. 4th ed. Upper Saddle River, NJ: Pearson.

MacGeorge, E. L. (2001). Support providers' interaction goals: the influence of attributions and emotions. *Communication Monographs*, 68, 72-97. doi: 10.1080/03637750128050.

MacGeorge, E. L., Feng, B., and Burleson, B. R. (2011). Supportive communication. In: M. L. Knapp, and J. A. Daly, eds., *Handbook of Interpersonal Communication*. Thousand Oaks, CA: Sage, pp. 317-354.

Matzat, U., and Snijders, C. (2012). Rebuilding trust in online shops on consumer review sites: Sellers' responses to user-generated complaints. *Journal of Computer-Mediated Communication*, 18, 62-79. doi: 10.1111/j.1083-6101.2012.01594.x.

McCullough, M. E., Kilpatrick, S. D., Emmons, R. A., and Larson, D. B. (2001). Is gratitude a moral affect? *Psychol Bull*, 127(2), 249-266. doi: http://dx.doi.org/10.1037/0033-2909.127.2.249.

Oshagan, H. (1996). Reference group influence on opinion expression. *International Journal of Public Opinion Research*, 8(4), 335-354. doi: 10.1093/ijpor/8.4.335.

Rains, S. A., Peterson, E. B., and Wright, K. B. (2015). Communicating social support in computer-mediated contexts: A meta-analytic review of content analyses examining support messages shared online among individuals coping with illness. *Communication Monographs*, 82(4), 403-430. doi: 10.1080/03637751.2015.1019530.

Scheufle, D. A., and Moy, P. (2000). Twenty-five years of the spiral of silence: A conceptual review and empirical outlook. *International Journal of Public Opinion Research*, 12(1), 3-28. doi: 10.1093/ijpor/12.1.3.

Stein, M. (1989). Gratitude and attitude: A note on emotional welfare. *Social Psychology Quarterly*, 52(3), 242-248. doi: 10.2307/2786719.

Tsang, J-A. (2006). Gratitude and prosocial behaviour: An experimental test of gratitude. *Cognition and Emotion*, 20, 138-148.

Chapter 4　Supportive Communication on Social Networking Sites: The Impact of Post Valence and Relational Closeness on Support Provision

Online supportive communication takes place on a variety of platforms. Online support forums primarily serve the function of support exchange and become the most popular platforms for online supportive communication. At the same time, other commonly used online venues, especially social networking sites (SNSs), have become an integral part of our everyday life and risen as a compelling venue for support seeking and provision (Meng et al., 2016). These platforms connect Internet users not only with close ones, but also with passing acquaintances (Ellison, Steinfield, Lampe, 2007; Rozzell et al., 2014). Taking advantage of a heterogenous network on SNSs, many people disclose their problems on these platforms and broadcast messages to a diverse audience. [1]

Although people are attracted by the convenience of SNSs to seek support, the effectiveness of these platforms is under debate (Vitak & Ellison, 2013). SNS users often disclose stressors and negative information in their support-seeking posts (Blight, Jagiello, Ruppel, 2015). These negative posts, however, are not much welcomed on SNSs (Waterloo et al., 2018). Research suggests that, on one hand, SNSs are guided by the norm of positivity bias in which positive broadcasts are viewed as more appropriate than negative ones (Reinecke & Trepte, 2014; Waterloo et al., 2018). People might be overwhelmed by too much negativity disclosed by a support-seeker (McLaughlin & Vitak, 2012). On the other hand, even

though people often disclose negative information in support-seeking posts
on SNSs (Blight, Jagiello, Ruppel, 2015), research about social support in
broader contexts shows that support-seeking can effectively elicit support
provision (Simpson et al., 2002). Additionally, individuals who seek more
support on SNSs perceive that they receive more support from other SNS
users (Oh, Lauckner, Boehmer, 2013). Therefore, disclosing personal
stressors for support-seeking may motivate others to offer help. Given the
different patterns revealed in research on SNSs and social support, it is
important to integrate literature in both fields to study supportive exchange on
SNSs. So far little has been done to examine whether and how post valence
would affect people's support provision on SNSs. This study strives to fill
this gap in literature by investigating the impact of a support-seeker's post
valence on others' intended support provision and the possible mechanisms
underlying the process.

A key feature of SNSs is a broad social network provided for users,
ranging from distant others to close friends (Rozzell et al., 2014). Although
broadcasting a support-seeking message to a wide audience enhances a
support-seeker's chance to be helped, the variations in relational closeness
may also complicate the process of supportive communication. Prior research
has offered some evidence showing that relational closeness affects people's
motivation to provide support on SNSs (Rains & Brunner, 2018). However, the
mechanisms under which relational closeness affects support provision on
SNSs have not been fully explored. Therefore, another objective of this
study is to examine whether and how relational closeness may influence
people's intended support provision on SNSs. In addition, this project
investigated if post valence and relational closeness would interact to affect
people's perceptions and appraisals of a support-seeker and their intention
to help.

This chapter reports two studies that investigate supportive communication
on SNSs. The first study was a pilot survey looking at people's use of SNSs
for supportive exchange in an ecological environment. The data enhanced

our understanding of the status quo of supportive exchange on SNSs. Built upon the pilot study, a main study experimentally examined the impact of post valence and relational closeness on people's perceptions of a support-seeker and their intended support provision on SNSs.

4.1 Posting Patterns and Social Support

SNSs serve as repositories of personal information and contain abundant cues reflecting users' identities and behaviors (Antheunis & Schouten, 2011). According to Brunswik's (1956) lens model, people can observe and perceive an individual based on cues available in the surrounding environment. Cues in a personal environment are selected and created by an individual and thus should reflect the individual's characteristics (Gosling et al., 2002). Gosling and his colleagues (Gosling et al., 2002) extended the lens model by specifying two types of cues crucial to the process of perception. *Identity claims* refer to information intentionally disclosed by a person to present themselves. *Behavioral residues* are cues unintentionally left in a personal environment which may reflect the individual's past or future behaviors.

Brunswik's (1956) lens model, especially its extension by Gosling and his colleagues (2002), has been applied to computer-mediated contexts such as SNSs (Antheunis & Schouten, 2011) and online support communities (Li & Feng, 2015; Rains et al., 2018). Self-generated cues such as status updates, photos, and self-descriptions are some of the most prevalent cues of identity claims. Other-generated (e. g., user comments) and system-generated (e. g., number of likes) cues are usually considered behavioral residues.

Posting patterns, as a type of identity claim, may serve as a lens to observe a poster's characteristics and influence observers' impressions of the poster. Research has found that frequency of posts altered people's impression of a poster, with frequent posters appearing more socially skilled and less depressed (Tokunaga & Quick, 2018). In addition, the

number of status updates has been shown to be positively related to posters'
openness to new experiences and extraversion (Bachrach et al. , 2012).

Post valence, despite being understudied, may provide another lens to
examine a poster's characteristics. Research suggests that people generally
adhere to the norm of positivity bias when using SNSs (Reinecke & Trepte,
2014; Waterloo et al. , 2018). Not only are most disclosures on SNSs
positive (Utz, 2015), but positive posts are also perceived more favorably
than negative posts (Reinecke & Trepte, 2014; Utz, 2015). People who
frequently disclose negative events on SNSs often receive undesirable or no
responses from the audience (Forest & Wood, 2012), likely due to people's
general tendency to dislike others who are pessimistic (Helweg-Larsen,
Sadeghian, Webb, 2002). Vogel, Rose, and Crane (2018) found that people
were more likely to provide support to positive posts than negative posts.
Likewise, High, Oeldorf-Hirsch, and Bellur (2014) found that SNS users
who disclose too much negative emotion received less support from
viewers. Although the underlying mechanism was not examined, they
postulated that negative disclosures on SNSs violated norms and might be
perceived negatively, leading to less support provision. This study attempts to
directly examine if posting more negative content may affect likeability of a
support-seeker and thus others' intended support provision. It is argued that a
person who posts more negative content may be perceived as less likeable
compared to someone who posts more positive content on SNSs.

Supportive communication literature has long recognized the fact that
people differed in their motivation to provide support (MacGeorge, Feng,
Burleson, 2011). Past research has found that the liking of a support-
seeker would positively affect others' online support provision (Li & Feng,
2015). People are more willing to provide support for others that they
like. Therefore, it is expected that valence of a support-seeker's previous
posts would affect others' liking of the support-seeker, and thus their
intended support provision.

H1: Compared to a support-seeker who posts mostly negative content on SNSs, a support-seeker who posts mostly positive content will be liked more, which in turn will positively affect people's intention to provide social support.

Post valence may also function through another concurrent mechanism to affect people's intention to provide social support. Valence of an individual's previous posts might be indicative of the negativity baseline of expression on SNSs. Those who frequently post negative posts may be perceived as having a relatively higher negativity baseline than those who post less negative content (Forest et al., 2014). Therefore, a support-seeking message from a frequent poster of negative content might be perceived as exaggerated and less indicative of a real need for support compared with a frequent poster of positive content. Forest and his colleagues (2014) conducted a series of studies and found some evidence to support the aforementioned rationale. Their results showed that high negativity baseline disclosers (i. e., those who frequently disclose negative content) would be perceived as having less support needs and would receive less support than low negativity baseline disclosers. Therefore, the following hypothesis is proposed.

H2: Compared to a support-seeker who posts mostly negative content on SNSs, a support-seeker who posts mostly positive content will be perceived to have a greater need for support, which in turn will positively affect people's intention to provide social support.

4.2 Relational Closeness and Social Support

SNSs have gradually shifted the ways people exchange support. The factor of relational closeness becomes more prominent in online supportive communication in part due to differences in audience accessibility and the degree of asynchronicity across channels. In face-to-face (FTF) communication, people often turn to strong ties, especially close friends and family members, for social support (Albrecht & Goldsmith, 2003). On SNSs, however, users can easily reach a broad audience varying in relational closeness, ranging from strangers to close friends (Carr, Wohn, Hayes, 2016). Further, the degree of asynchronicity prevalent in online interactions also makes relational closeness more relevant in online support provision versus FTF supportive communication. The simultaneous nature of FTF interaction drives people to respond to a support-seeking request in real time, regardless of relational closeness. In addition, asynchronous public channels on SNSs afford people more freedom to respond or not to a support-seeking post. In fact, staying mute or lurking on SNSs usually goes unnoticed and comes with little social consequences. Many viewers, especially those who are not close to a poster, may not feel obligated to respond to a support-seeking post disseminated to an undifferentiated audience (Rains & Keating, 2011). Due to the salient role of relational closeness in SNSs, this project attempted to examine if and how relational closeness would affect people's perceptions of a support-seeker and their intention to provide support.

Liking has been long recognized as a defining feature of relational closeness (Bukowski, Motzoi, Meyer, 2012). Interpersonal relationships vary in closeness and differ in the level of liking. For example, friendship is rooted in mutual liking, whereas acquaintances typically do not share high levels of positive affect such as liking and intimacy. SNSs consist of relationships varying in closeness, including but not limited to close friends, casual friends, and acquaintances. A recent study examining online supportive exchange showed a positive association between perceived closeness and the liking of a support-seeker (Rains & Brunner, 2018). People like others who share a close relationship. It is thus expected that people will like a close friend more than an acquaintance who seeks support on SNSs. Liking in turn may motivate people to provide more support (Li & Feng, 2015). Therefore, the following hypothesis is proposed.

H3: Compared to an acquaintance, a close friend will be liked more, which in turn will positively affect people's intention to provide social support.

Besides liking, relational closeness may affect people's appraisals of a support-seeker's support needs. Research shows that people have the tendency to include close others in their self-concept and have a self-serving bias when making attributions about close others' behaviors (Aron & Aron, 1997; Heider, 1958; Taifel & Turner, 1979). That is, negative events happening to oneself and close others are often attributed to situational factors, whereas the same events happening to less close others are more likely ascribed to dispositions and personal characteristics. The self-serving bias may thus lead people to think a close other is not at fault for the stressor and is in real need of support, whereas a less close other holding more personal responsibilities for the stressor, is blameworthy, and is in less need of support. The appraisal of an individual's support needs may in turn affect others' motivation to provide support.

H4: Compared to an acquaintance, a close friend will be perceived to have a greater need for support, which in turn will positively affect people's intention to provide social support.

In addition to the main effects from post valence and relational closeness on people's perceptions of a support-seeker and their intention to help, this study also attempted to explore an interaction effect between post valence and relational closeness on perceptual outcomes and behavioral intentions. Through several independent studies, Forest et al. (2014) found that post valence would significantly affect people's appraisals of a support-seeker's needs and their responsiveness in close relationships. Compared with a romantic partner that has a low negativity baseline, a romantic partner with a high negativity baseline would be perceived to have a lower need for support and receive less support. This pattern, however, was not found in another study examining non-close relationships. In addition, Rains and Brunner's (2018) work showed some evidence that the influence of post valence on liking and people's willingness to provide support would be contingent on relational closeness. Although they did not directly examine the interaction effect between post valence and relational closeness on the outcome variables, their analyses showed that the relative impact of negative disclosures (compared to positive disclosures) on liking and intended support provision would be greater among acquaintances than among close friends. Because research evidence is relatively limited, the following research question is raised.

RQ1: Will valence of previous posts interact with relational closeness to affect (a) people's liking of a support-seeker and (b) their appraisals of the seeker's support need, and thereby (c) their intention to provide support?

4.3 Pilot Study: Exploring the Use of SNSs for Supportive Exchange

A polit study was conducted to (a) examine if relational closeness would be associated with the likelihood of responding to a support-seeking post in an ecological environment and (b) identify the most popular SNS platforms that people use for supportive exchange. Using a survey method, this study examined how people use SNSs to exchange support with acquaintances and close friends. Upon arrival in the lab, each participant was instructed to log onto the SNS that they most frequently visit and to identify the two most recent support-seeking posts, one from an acquaintance and the other from a close friend. Specifically, participants were asked to identify posts in which they tried to seek comfort or help in the face of difficulties and stressors. Any posts that did not meet the requirements were excluded from data analysis. They were then asked to answer questions about whether or not they replied to the support-seeking post, the posting platform, and their usage of SNSs.

A total of 277 students who attended a Midwest university in the US participated in this study for extra credit. 147 (53.1%) participants (Age: $M = 20.79$, $SD = 1.93$) were able to provide two qualified support-seeking posts and were included in the final analysis. The final sample consisted of 71.1% female ($n = 106$) and 28.9% male ($n = 41$). Most participants identified themselves as Caucasian/European/White ($n = 109$, 74.1%), followed by Asian or Asian American ($n = 17$, 11.6%,), other racial/ethnic groups ($n = 12$, 8.2%), and African American ($n = 9$, 6.1%).

Overall, the three most popular platforms identified in this study were Facebook ($n = 119$, 40.5%), Twitter ($n = 118$, 40.1%), and Instagram ($n = 48$, 16.3%). Channel popularity slightly differed as a function of relational closeness. Most messages posted by close friends were from Facebook ($n = 68$, 45.9%), Twitter ($n = 51$, 34.5%), and Instagram ($n = 24$, 16.2%). Most messages posted by acquaintances were from Twitter ($n = 67$, 45.3%), Facebook ($n = 51$, 34.5%), and Instagram ($n = 24$, 16.2%).

In addition, a majority of participants reported that they did not reply to acquaintances ($n = 132$, 89.2%) and close friends ($n = 114$, 77.0%). See Table 4.1 for more detail. A mixed logistic regression model using R 3.3.2 showed that relational closeness affected people's tendency to reply to the posts they provided. The odds ratio of replying to a post from a close friend was about four times larger than that from an acquaintance, $b = 1.40$, OR $= 4.05$, $p = 0.005$, after controlling for posting channel, post word count, and time spent on SNSs.

Table 4.1   Counts of replies/no replies to a support-seeking post in study 1

Case	Reply	No reply	Total
Acquaintance	15	132	147
Close friend	33	114	147
Total	48	246	294

Although people are provided a wide selection of SNSs for supportive exchange, the results showed that Facebook was the top choice, followed by Twitter and Instagram. Moreover, this study offered some evidence that relational closeness was positively associated with people's support provision on SNSs. People replied more often to a close friend's support-seeking post compared to an acquaintance's post.

4.4 The Main Study: An Experiment on Support Seeking and Provision on SNSs

The main study experimentally examined the impact of post valence and relational closeness on people's perceptions of a support-seeker and their intention to provide support on SNSs. Specifically, this study manipulated valence of a support-seeker's previous posts and relational closeness. Because the pilot study revealed that supportive exchanges are most often found on Facebook, Facebook was chosen as the main platform to further examine online support in this experiment.

4.4.1 Participants

A total of 337 participants aged 18 or older were recruited from the same university as those in study 1. Respondents participated in exchange for extra credit. 92 cases were excluded from data analysis because these participants failed either attention check questions ($n = 12$, 3.56%) or manipulation check questions ($n = 80$, 23.74%). Therefore, responses from 245 valid participants, aged 19 to 48 ($M = 22.22$, $SD = 3.59$), were used in the final analysis. Of these participants, 66.53% ($n = 163$) identified themselves as male, and 33.47% ($n = 82$) identified as female. Most participants considered themselves to be Caucasian/European/White ($n = 171$, 69.8%), followed by Asian/Asian-American ($n = 38$, 15.5%), African/African-American/Black ($n = 23$, 9.4%), Latino ($n = 8$, 3.3%), and other racial/ethnic groups ($n = 5$, 2.0%).

4.4.2 Experimental Design

A lab experiment employing a 2 (relational closeness: close friend vs. acquaintance) × 2 (valence of previous posts: positive vs. negative) × 2 (post topic: home life vs. school life) between-subjects factorial design was conducted. This study used Facebook webpages displaying mock-up status updates for a person named Alex. Each of the webpages displayed the update(s) made by Alex on a single day of the week. Participants were instructed to read some background information about Alex, review all eight status updates spanning five days, and respond to questions based on the last post (i.e., the support-seeking post). Half of the messages were adapted and modified from Rains and Brunner's (2018) study, and the other half were written by the authors after reading SNS users' status updates collected from another unpublished study.

Similar to Rains and Brunner's (2018) study, relational closeness was manipulated by describing the poster Alex as a close friend or an acquaintance of the same age, the same sex, and as a current resident of the same town as the participant. Close friend Alex was described as someone the participant knew from college and frequently interacted with. Acquaintance Alex was depicted as someone the participant met at a friend's dinner party and did not interact with very often.

Valence of previous posts was manipulated through the valence of the other seven status updates (i.e., the status updates prior to the support-seeking post) posted on the first four days (i.e., Monday through Thursday). Positive posts generally reflected optimistic thoughts, exciting experiences, and positive energy. Negative posts displayed pessimistic thoughts, unfortunate experiences, and discouragement. The positive posts condition consisted of six positive posts and one neutral post. The negative posts condition mixed six negative posts and one neutral post (Table 4.2). A neutral post was included in all conditions to increase the realism of the stimuli. Efforts were made to keep the length of posts comparable across conditions. Only antonyms of a few key words were used to modify the valence of a post. An example of a positive post was "Just watched an awesome movie." The negative version was "Just watched a terrible movie." The last post on the fifth day was the support-seeking post asking participants about their intended support. Therefore, the last post did not differ in its valence across conditions.

Table 4.2   Sample positive and negative posts focused on home life in study 2

Condition	Monday	Tuesday	Wednesday	Thursday	Friday (i.e., The support-seeking post)
Positive	All moved into my new place. I think I'm going to love it.	Had mac and cheese with dinner tonight.	What a good day. Just trying to figure out plans for this weekend.	Raining this morning. LOVE the rain!	Feeling down today.
		Just finished watching the game. Three hours of complete excitement.		Working out is so much fun than I expected.	
				Just watched an awesome movie.	
Negative	All moved into my new place. I think I'm going to hate it.	Had mac and cheese with dinner tonight.	What a terrible day. Just trying to figure out plans for this weekend.	Raining this morning. HATE the rain!	Feeling down today.
		Just finished watching the game. Three hours of complete let down.		Working out way more boring than I expected.	
				Just watched a terrible movie.	

To ensure that results were not an artifact of any specific topic, this study included two topics focusing on either home life or school life. The first set of status updates mostly pertained to home life such as leisure activities (e. g., "Just finished watching the game. Three hours of complete let down."). The second set of posts emphasized school-relevant issues such as coursework (e. g., "This course is so much fun. A good use of my time.").

After viewing the seven posts manipulated in valence, every participant was exposed to a support-seeking message posted on Friday. To ensure that results were not due to specific posts, two different support-seeking posts were respectively included in the two sets of post topics. In the school life topic condition, the support-seeking post was "Feeling emotionally drained today." In the home life topic condition, the support-seeking post was "Feeling lonely today." Participants were then asked to answer questions based on the support-seeking post and the poster.

4.4.3 Measures

Perceived liking. To determine personal liking of a support-seeker, a scale of eight items adapted from Li and Feng's (2015) study was used to measure this variable. The items were measured on a 7-point Likert-scale (1 = *strongly disagree*, 7 = *strongly agree*). Example items were "Alex is a likeable person," "Alex is pleasant to be with," and "I could never establish a personal friendship with Alex." The scores on all items were averaged to obtain a mean ($M = 3.78$, $SD = 0.95$, Cronbach's $a = 0.89$).

Perceived need for support. Five items on a 7-point Likert-scale (1 = *strongly disagree*, 7 = *strongly agree*) were used to assess people's appraisal of a poster's need for support ($M = 4.92$, $SD = 0.95$). Due to a lack of established measures of this variable, some items have been developed based on existing literature (Forest et al., 2014). Example items were "I think Alex needs much support" and "I think Alex needs comfort or reassurance." An exploratory factor analysis was conducted on the five items. Only one component had an eigenvalue over 1 and explained 59.17% of the variance. All items had loading values greater than 0.60. The reliability test of the five items indicated the measure had a satisfactory reliability, Cronbach's $\alpha = 0.82$.

Intended support provision. Participants' willingness to provide emotional support was assessed using five items on a 7-point Likert-scale (1 = *strongly disagree*, 7 = *strongly agree*; $M = 4.84$, $SD = 1.29$, $a = 0.90$) modified from Xu and Burleson's scale (Xu & Burleson, 2001). Sample items were

"I would sympathize with the poster" and "I would express understanding of the situation that is bothering the poster."

4. 4. 4 Control Variables

Perceived realism. The perceived realism scale was adapted from Li and Zhang's study (2018). It asked participants to rate three items on a 7-point Likert-scale (1 = *strongly disagree*, 7 = *strongly agree*; $M = 5.69$, $SD = 0.94$, $a = 0.81$). The items were "All the posts described something that could happen in real life," "The set of posts portrayed a possible real-life situation," and "The whole set of posts is realistic and believable."

Participant's sex. Because previous research suggested that sex could influence people's support provision (Samter, 2002), participant's sex was also included as a control variable. Participant's sex was rated on one item "What is your sex" (0 = *male*, 1 = *female*). Of these participants, 66.53% ($n = 163$) were self-identified as male and 33.47% ($n = 82$) as female.

4. 4. 5 Manipulation Checks

Relationship closeness. Each participant was asked to check if Alex was described as a close friend or an acquaintance in this scenario. A total of 70 participants (20.77%) failed this question and were excluded from the final analysis.

Valence of previous posts. Participants were also asked whether most status updates were positive or negative. Those who did not correctly identify the valence of previous posts ($n = 10$, 2.97%) were excluded from the final analysis.

4.5 Results

T-tests were first conducted to examine if perceived liking, perceived need for support, and intended support provision would differ by the two post topics. The results did not reveal significant differences on any of the three measures across the two post topics ($p \geqslant 0.202$). The statistical analysis program PROCESS version 3.4 was used to test the mediation and moderated mediation effects in the hypotheses. PROCESS is a regression-based path analytic tool for estimating direct and indirect effects in mediation and moderation models (Hayes, 2018). All hypotheses were simultaneously tested with Model 8 in PROCESS. Post valence was entered as the independent variable, relational closeness as the moderator, liking and perceived need for support as two parallel mediators, and intended support provision as the dependent variable. Post topics, perceived realism, and participant sex were included as control variables. The symbols a, b, and ab reported below represented unstandardized regression coefficients. Means and standard deviations of outcome variables by condition are provided in Table 4.3. Figure 4.1 displays all paths tested in the hypotheses.

Table 4.3 Means and standard deviations of outcome variables by condition in study 2

Variabes	Acquaintance		Close friend	
	Negative posts ($n = 76$)	Positive posts ($n = 63$)	Negative posts ($n = 54$)	Positive posts ($n = 52$)
Liking	3.25 (0.80)	4.11 (0.78)	3.56 (0.84)	4.39 (0.96)
Need for support	5.06 (0.91)	4.65 (0.86)	5.30 (0.91)	4.63 (0.99)
Willingness to provide support	3.05 (1.76)	2.83 (1.54)	3.55 (1.97)	3.99 (2.05)

Note: Standard deviations are in parentheses.

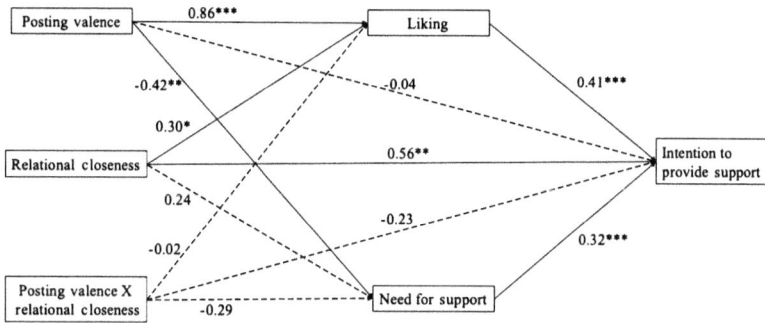

Figure 4.1   All paths in the tested hypotheses

Note: Solid lines represent significant paths; dotted lines represent
nonsignificant paths. * $p<0.05$. ** $p<0.01$. *** $p<0.001$.

H1 proposed that compared with a support-seeker who posted more
negative content, a support-seeker who posted more positive content would
be perceived as more likeable, and people would be more willing to provide
support to this person. As predicted, results showed that people perceived
a poster of more positive content as more likeable ($M = 4.24$, $SD = 0.88$)
than a poster of more negative content ($M = 3.38$, $SD = 0.83$; $a = 0.86$,
$SE = 0.14$, $t = 5.997$, $p<0.001$). Liking in turn positively affected
intended support provision ($b = 0.41$, $SE = 0.09$, $t = 4.77$, $p<0.001$).
The mediation effect was confirmed by 5,000 resampling bootstrapping
tests, and the finding held regardless of whether a support-seeking post was
from an acquaintance ($ab = 0.36$; $SE = 0.10$, 95% CI $= 0.1775-0.5665$) or
from a close friend ($ab = 0.35$; $SE = 0.12$, 95% CI $= 0.1521-0.6114$).
Therefore, H1 was supported.

H2 predicted that a poster of more positive content would be perceived
to have a greater need for support than a poster of more negative content
and would likely receive more support. Contrary to the prediction, people
perceived a poster of more positive content ($M = 4.65$, $SD = 0.09$) to have
lower need for support than a poster of more negative content ($M = 5.16$,
$SD = 0.08$; $a = -0.42$, $SE = 0.16$, $t = -2.68$, $p = 0.008$), although

perceived need for support positively affected people's intention to provide support as predicted ($b = 0.32$, $SE = 0.08$, $t = 4.00$, $p<0.001$). Despite the findings regarding valence and perceived need for support, the indirect effect was confirmed by 5,000 resampling bootstrapping tests for both acquaintances ($ab = -0.13$; $SE = 0.07$, 95% CI $= -0.2950$–0.0253) and close friends ($ab = -0.23$; $SE = 0.09$, 95% CI $= -0.4357$–0.0708). People perceived a poster of more positive content to have a lower need for support than a poster of more negative content, and thus they had less intention to provide support. H2 was not supported.

H3 proposed that liking would mediate the relationship between relational closeness and intention to provide support. As predicted, people liked a close friend ($M = 3.97$, $SD = 0.99$) more than an acquaintance ($M = 3.64$, $SD = 0.90$; $a = 0.30$, $SE = 0.15$, $t = 2.004$, $p = 0.046$), and thus intended to provide more support to the close friend ($b = 0.41$, $SE = 0.09$, $t = 4.77$, $p<0.001$). The indirect effect was confirmed by 5,000 resampling bootstrapping tests, $ab = 0.09$; $SE = 0.05$, 95% CI $= 0.0176$–0.1962. Therefore, H3 was supported.

H4 hypothesized that relational closeness would positively affect perceived need for support and thus intention to provide support. A close friend ($M = 4.97$, $SD = 0.10$) was not perceived to be of greater need for support than an acquaintance ($M = 4.87$, $SD = 0.08$; $a = 0.24$, $SE = 0.16$, $t = 1.49$, $p = 0.136$), although greater need for support led to intention to provide higher quality support ($b = 0.32$, $SE = 0.08$, $t = 4.00$, $p<0.001$). The 5,000 resampling bootstrapping tests also showed the indirect effect was not significant, $ab = 0.03$; $SE = 0.05$, 95% CI $= -0.0526$–0.1319. H4 was not supported.

The research question examined the interaction effect between post valence and relational closeness on intended support provision through liking and need for support. The results showed that the interaction between post valence and relational closeness did not significantly affect liking ($a = -0.02$, $SE = 0.22$, $t = -0.10$, $p = 0.921$), perceived need for support ($a =$

-0.29, $SE = 0.24$, $t = -1.22$, $p = 0.225$), or intended support provision ($a = -0.23$, $SE = 0.29$, $t = -0.78$, $p = 0.437$).

4.6 Discussion

This project examined the underlying mechanisms through which contextual and relational cues affect people's intention to provide social support on SNSs. The pilot study examined the status quo of people's supportive exchange on SNSs, and the main study experimentally examined if and how valence of previous posts and relational closeness affect viewers' perceptions of a support-seeker and their intention to provide support. Results suggested that valence of previous posts positively affected people's liking of a support-seeker and their intention to provide support. However, valence of previous posts negatively impacts the appraisal of a support-seeker's need, which in turn impacts intended support provision. In addition, people perceive a close friend as more likeable than an acquaintance and become more willing to provide support for the former.

This project contributes to the online support literature by examining the influence of post valence on people's perceptions of a support-seeker and their intention to provide support. As an identity cue, post valence so far has only received limited attention in research on social support (Rains & Brunner, 2018). This project extends the applicability of the norm of positivity bias to the domain of social support. The results confirm the norm of positivity bias by showing that people who frequently post positive content on SNSs are more likeable than those who frequently post negative content. Liking is a prominent motivation for social support and drives people to provide more social support to likeable individuals. Future research can extend this line of work by examining the valence of a support-seeking post. Buehler's (2017) study revealed that people sometimes include positive content (e.g., optimism) in a support-seeking message on SNSs. According to the norm of positivity bias, such content may also lead to a more favorable perception of a support-seeker and perhaps elicit more support.

Contrary to the prediction, a frequent poster of negative content was perceived to have a greater need for support and thus received more support than a frequent poster of positive content. Although this finding goes against the conclusions in Forest et al. (2014), it is consistent with sensitive interactions systems theory (Barbee & Cunningham, 1995). According to this theory, people use indirect methods to indicate support needs and to seek support. For example, a support-seeker may complain about a situation or hint that a problem exists without explicitly asking for help. Frequently posting negative content may indicate that the individual indeed experiences stressors and needs help. Further, although several studies in Forest et al. 's (2014) work found a positive impact of post valence on perceived need for support, their first experiment failed to find such an impact. This experiment asked participants to review ostensible undergraduate student Alicia's status updates on Facebook and answer questions about their perceptions of Alicia and their responsiveness to her last post. The results found that positive valence did not affect need for support or willingness to respond. The researchers postulated that lacking prior interaction made it difficult for participants to assess Alicia's stress level, and participants would have little motivation to respond to a stranger. This study improved Forest et al. 's (2014) manipulation by presenting Alex as an acquaintance or a close friend with the appropriate background displayed. Given that participants are college students who share similar backgrounds with the support-seeker in the experiment, they are more likely to feel the stressors indicated by the support-seeker in the negative posts, sympathize with the seeker, and be willing to provide support. Alternatively, the result aligns with the self-presentational dilemma that individuals face in support-seeking. As shown in previous studies (Silver, Wortman, Crofton, 1990), presentation of positive coping with life distress fails to indicate desire for support, which cannot elicit efficacious support. Due to the competing findings found in this project and previous research, future research should try to reconcile the conflict by further examining the impact of post valence on need for support and intention to provide support with different research methods and across diverse contexts.

The results from this project show that post valence works as a double-edged sword to affect people's intention to provide support on SNSs. On one hand, posting more positive content may increase others' liking of a support-seeker; on the other hand, people may perceive a frequent poster of positive content to have lower need for support. A close look at the results suggests that post valence has a stronger impact on liking than on need for support, and subsequently on people's intention to provide support. In other words, the positive impact of post valence on liking may override its negative impact on need for support. Taken together, a support-seeker who frequently posts positive content is likely to receive more support than a frequent poster of negative content. At the same time, considering the positive impact of perceived need for support on support intention, support-seekers may employ other strategies rather than posting negative content to indicate their strong need for support. For example, sensitive interactions systems theory (Barbee & Cunningham, 1995) suggests that people can use direct strategies to seek support, such as explicitly asking for help. According to the theory, direct support-seeking strategies can help people better appraise the need for support and thus work better than indirect strategies in eliciting support.

In addition to post valence, this project also examined the impact of relational closeness on intended support provision and two possible underlying mechanisms. People differ in their motivation to help a target, in part due to their closeness with the target. Given the relational nuances presented on SNSs, it is surprising to find out that only a handful of work has looked at relational closeness in supportive communication on SNSs. The limited body of research mostly examined the impact of relational closeness on supportive exchange from the perspective of a support-seeker. That is, they examined if relational closeness affects the perceived effectiveness of social support (Carr, Wohn, Hayes, 2016). Apart from prior research, this project investigated the influence of relational closeness on support provision from the perspective of a support-provider. The lack of research from this perspective might be related to methodological challenges. It is relatively difficult to manipulate relational closeness in an ecologically valid way. To address this problem, the current project adopted methods used in Rains and Brunner's (2018) research by conducting both a pilot survey and an experiment to complement one another and to enhance internal and external validity of the results. The survey study gave participants opportunities to reflect on their relational closeness with a support-seeker in a natural setting. The controlled experiment helped identify causal relationships between relational closeness and intended support provision. The two studies collectively showed that relational closeness between a support-seeker and a viewer would positively influence the viewer's support provision. More importantly, this project filled a gap in the online support literature by considering the impact of relational closeness on psychological outcomes (i. e., liking, perceived need for support) related to intended support provision. This project found that relational closeness positively affected intended support provision through liking; however, the mediating effect of need for support was not significant. It appears that people do not consider friends experiencing stress to be in need of more support than acquaintances. It is possible that people rely on cues available on SNSs to infer a seeker's need for support instead of exercising the self-serving bias when they make such appraisals. These results present some practical suggestions to support-seekers on SNSs. For users who are concerned about privacy and do not want to share their support-seeking messages with everyone on SNSs, choosing a group of close friends with whom to share the message may be just as effective as sharing it with an undifferentiated audience.

This project did not find a significant interaction effect between post valence and relational closeness on liking and thus support provision. The difference in results found in this project compared to Rains and Brunner's work (2018) could be explained by the different analyses conducted in the two studies. Rains and Brunner (2018) conducted a series of t-tests to examine the discrepancy between positive and negative disclosure conditions for liking and intended support provision. The current project directly examined the interaction between post valence and relational closeness on the outcome variables. Future research could try to incorporate both analyses in one study to further explore the possible interaction effect.

This project has several limitations that present opportunities for future research. First, a student sample may limit the generalization of results to other populations. Although college students emerge as one of the most prominent groups to use SNSs, these platforms attract users of all backgrounds who may exhibit different supportive communication patterns. Replicating the studies with a non-student sample may help test the generalizability of these results.

Second, participants in the main study were asked to imagine Alex as a close friend or an acquaintance based on information provided in the vignette. Because participants did not engage in actual interaction with Alex, it is somewhat difficult to consider Alex as a close friend or an acquaintance. Therefore, a few participants failed the manipulation check on relational closeness. The manipulation of relational closeness could be further enhanced by considering emotional attachment, need fulfillment, and irreplaceability which are characteristics of close relationships. Despite the limitations, a manipulation of relational closeness helped to isolate other factors and assess the causal relationships between relational closeness and intended support provision (Rains & Brunner, 2018). In addition, a survey study on relational closeness was first conducted to enhance the external validity.

Third, it is worthwhile to note that Facebook was used as an exemplar of SNSs in the current project. The use of Facebook was based on results in the pilot study. It is acknowledged that different SNSs possess different affordances (Fox & McEwan, 2017) and could have distinct influences on the process of supportive communication. Nevertheless, the two factors examined in this project-post valence and relational closeness are common features present on most SNSs. Future research could explore the impact of other SNS cues on supportive exchange and further develop this body of research.

4.7 Conclusion

SNSs provide people with an appealing channel to seek and provide social support. Users can easily broadcast their support-seeking messages to a diverse audience. However, support-seeking on SNSs may not always lead to effective support provision. SNS users tend to adhere to the norm of positivity bias in that they perceive a frequent poster of positive content to be more likeable than a frequent poster of negative content, and as a result, intend to provide higher quality support for the former. In addition, a frequent poster of negative content can be perceived to be in greater need of support than a frequent poster of positive content. The appraisal of support need in turn positively affects people's intention to provide support. Future research should continue to explore the social implications of SNSs on supportive communication, and more importantly, help SNS users to more effectively exchange support on these platforms.

Note

1. A version of this chapter has been published as: Li, S., and Zhang, G. (2021). Supportive communication on social networking sites: The impact of post valence and relational closeness on support provision. *Telematics and Informatics*, 63, 101.

References

Albrecht, T. L., and Goldsmith, D. J. (2003). Social support, social networks, and health. In: T. L. Thompson, A. M. Dorsey, K. I. Miller, and R. Parrott, eds., *Handbook of Health Communication*. Mahwah, NJ: Lawrence Erlbaum Associates Publishers, pp. 263-284.

Antheunis, M. L., and Schouten, A. P. (2011). The effects of other-generated and system-generated cues on adolescents' perceived attractiveness on social network sites. *Journal of Computer-Mediated Communication*, 16, 391-406. doi: 10.1111/j.1083-6101.2011.01545.x.

Aron, A., and Aron, E. N. (1997). Self-expansion motivation and including other in the self. In: S. Duck, ed., *Handbook of personal relationships: Theory, Research, and Intervention*. 2nd ed. Chichester, England: John Wiley & Sons Inc, pp. 251-270.

Barbee, A. P., and Cunningham, M. R. (1995). An experimental approach to social support communications: Interactive coping in close relationships. In: B. R. Burleson, ed., *Communication Yearbook* 18. Thousand Oaks, CA: Sage, pp. 381-413.

Blight, M. G., Jagiello, K., and Ruppel, E. K. (2015). "Same stuff different day:" A mixed-method study of support seeking on Facebook. *Computers in Human Behavior*, 53, 366-373. doi: https://doi.org/10.1016/j.chb.2015.07.029.

Brunswik, E. (1956). *Perception and the Representative Design of Psychological Experiments*. Berkeley, CA: University of California Press.

Buehler, E. M. (2017). "You shouldn't use facebook for that": Navigating norm violations while seeking emotional support on Facebook. *Social Media + Society*, 3, 1-11. doi: 10.1177/2056305117733225.

Bukowski, W. M., Motzoi, C., and Meyer, F. (2012). Friendship as process, function, and outcome. In: K. H. Rubin, W. M. Bukowski, and B. Laursen, eds., *Handbook of Peer Interactions, Relationships,* and Groups. New York: The Guilford Press, pp. 217-231.

Carr, C. T., Wohn, D. Y., and Hayes, R. A. (2016). As social support: Relational closeness, automaticity, and interpreting social support from paralinguistic digital affordances in social media. *Computers in Human Behavior*, 62, 385-393. doi: http://dx.doi.org/10.1016/j.chb.2016. 03.087.

Ellison, N. B., Steinfield, C., and Lampe, C. (2007). The benefits of Facebook "friends": Social capital and college students' use of online social network sites. *Journal of Computer-Mediated Communication*, 12, 1143-1168. doi: 10.1111/j.1083-6101.2007.00367.x.

Forest, A. L., Kille, D. R., Wood, J. V., and Holmes, J. G. (2014). Discount and disengage: How chronic negative expresivity undermines partner responsiveness to negative disclosures. *Journal of Personality and Social Psycholigy*, 107, 1013-1032. doi: 10.1037/a0038163.

Forest, A. L., and Wood, J. V. (2012). When social networking is not working: Individuals with low self-esteem recognize but do not reap the benefits of self-disclosure on Facebook. *Psychological Science*, 23, 295-302. doi: 10.1177/0956797611429709.

Fox, J., and McEwan, B. (2017). Distinguishing technologies for social interaction: The perceived social affordances of communication channels scale. *Communication Monographs*, 84, 298-318. doi: 10.1080/0363 7751.2017.1332418.

Gosling, S. D., Ko, S. J., Mannarelli, T., and Morris, M. E. (2002). A room with a cue: Personality judgments based on offices and bedrooms. *Journal of Personality Social Psychology*, 82, 379-398. doi: 10.1037//0022-3514.82.3.379.

Hayes, A. F. (2018). *Introduction to Mediation, Moderation, and Conditional Process Analysis: A Regression-Based Approach*. 2nd ed. New York: The Guilford Press.

Heider, F. (1958). The Psychology of Interpersonal Relations. New York: John Wiley & Sons.

Helweg-Larsen, M., Sadeghian, P., and Webb, M. S. (2002). The stigma of being pessimistically biased. *Journal of Social and Clinical Psychology*, 21, 92-107. doi: 10.1521/jscp.21.1.92.22405v.

High, A. C., Oeldorf-Hirsch, A., and Bellur, S. (2014). Misery rarely gets company: The influence of emotional bandwidth on supportive communication on Facebook. *Computers in Human Behavior*, 34, 79-88. doi: 10.1016/j.chb.2014.01.037.

Li, S., and Feng, B. (2015). What to say to an online support-seeker?: The influence of others' responses and support-seekers' replies. *Human Communication Research*, 41, 303-326. doi: 10.1111/hcre.12055.

Li, S., and Zhang, G. (2018). Intergroup communication in online forums: The effect of group identification on online support provision. *Communication Research*, 48(6), 874-894. doi: 10.1177/0093650 218807041.

MacGeorge, E. L., Feng, B., and Burleson, B. R. (2011). Supportive Communication. In: M. L. Knapp, and J. A. Daly, eds., *Handbook of Interpersonal Communication*. Thousand Oaks, CA: Sage, pp. 317-354.

McLaughlin, C., and Vitak, J. (2012). Norm evolution and violation on Facebook. *New Media & Society*, 14, 299-315. doi: 10.1177/1461444 811412712.

Meng, J., Martinez, L., Holmstrom, A., Chung, M., and Cox, J. (2016). Research on social networking sites and social support from 2004 to 2015: A narrative review and directions for future research. *Cyberpsychology, Behavior, and Social Networking*, 20, 44-51. doi: 10.1089/cyber.2016.0325.

Oh, H. J., Lauckner, C., and Boehmer, J. (2013). Facebooking for health: An examination into the solicitation and effects of health-related social support on social networking sites. *Computers in Human Behavior*, 29, 2072-2080. doi: 10.1016/j.chb.2013.04.017.

Rains, S. A., and Brunner, S. R. (2018). The outcomes of broadcasting self-disclosure using new communication technologies: Responses to disclosure vary across one's social network. *Communication Research*, 45, 659-687. doi: 10.1177/0093650215598836.

Rains, S. A., and Keating, D. M. (2011). The social dimension of blogging about health: Health blogging, social support, and well-being. *Communication Monographs*, 78, 511-534. doi: 10.1080/03637751. 2011.618142.

Rains, S. A., Tsetsi, E., Akers, C., Pavlich, C. A., and Appelbaum, M. (2018). Factors influencing the quality of social support messages produced online: The role of responsibility for distress and others' support attempts. *Communication Research*, 46(6), 866-886. doi: 10. 1177/0093650218796371.

Reinecke, L., and Trepte, S. (2014). Authenticity and well-being on social network sites: A two-wave longitudinal study on the effects of online authenticity and the positivity bias in SNS communication. *Computers in Human Behavior*, 30, 95-102. doi: 10.1016/j.chb. 2013.07.030.

Rozzell, B., Piercy, C. W., Carr, C. T., King, S., Lane, B. L., Tornes, M., and Wright, K. B. (2014). Notification pending: Online social support from close and nonclose relational ties via Facebook. *Computers in Human Behavior*, 38, 272-280. doi: 10. 1016/j.chb.2014.06.006.

Samter, W. (2002). How gender and cognitive complexity influence the provision of emotional support: A study of indirect effects. *Communication Reports*, 15, 5-16. doi: 10.1080/08934210209367748.

Silver, R. C., Wortman, C. B., and Crofton, C. (1990). The role of coping in support provision: The self-presentational dilemma of victims of life crises. In: B. R. Sarason, I. G. Sarason, and G. R. Pierce, eds., *Social Support: An Interactional View*. New York: John Wiley & Sons, pp. 397-426.

Simpson, J. A., Rholes, W. S., Oriña, M. M., and Grich, J. (2002). Working models of attachment, support giving, and support seeking in a stressful situation. *Personality and Social Psychology Bulletin*, 28, 598-608. doi: 10.1177/0146167202288004.

Tajfel, H., and Turner, J. C. (1979). An integrative theory of intergroup conflict. In: W. G. Austin and S. Worchel, eds., *The Social Psychology of Intergroup Relations*. Monterey, CA: Brooks-Cole, pp. 33-47.

Tokunaga, R. S., and Quick, J. D. (2018). Impressions on social networking sites: Examining the influence of frequency of status updates and likes on judgments of observers. *Media Psychology*, 21, 157-181. doi: 10.1080/15213269.2017.1282874.

Utz, S. (2015). The function of self-disclosure on social network sites: Not only intimate, but also positive and entertaining self-disclosures increase the feeling of connection. *Computers in Human Behavior*, 45, 1-10. doi: 10.1016/j.chb.2014.11.076.

Vitak, J., and Ellison, N. B. (2013). "There's a network out there you might as well tap": Exploring the benefits of and barriers to exchanging informational and support-based resources on Facebook. *New Media & Society*, 15, 243-259. doi: 10.1177/1461444812451566.

Vogel, E. A., Rose, J. P., and Crane, C. (2018). "Transformation Tuesday": Temporal context and post valence influence the provision of social support on social media. *The Journal of Social Psychology*, 158, 446-459. doi: 10.1080/00224545.2017.1385444.

Waterloo, S. F., Baumgartner, S. E., Peter, J., and Valkenburg, P. M. (2018). Norms of online expressions of emotion: Comparing Facebook, Twitter, Instagram, and WhatsApp. *New Media & Society*, 20, 1813-1831. doi: 10.1177/1461444817707349.

Xu, Y., and Burleson, B. R. (2001). Effects of sex, culture, and support type on perceptions of spousal social support: An assessment of the "support gap" hypothesis in early marriage. *Human Communication Research*, 27, 535-566. doi: 10.1111/j.1468-2958.2001.tb00792.x.

Chapter 5　Different Forms of Support Provision on Social Network Sites

Social network sites are popular platforms for supportive communication (Rains & Wright, 2016). While publicness on SNSs affords users a way to conveniently reach a large audience and thus enhance the likelihood of receiving help (Carr, Wohn, Hayes, 2016), self-presentational concerns may constrain the way that people seek support on SNSs (Oh & LaRose, 2016). How people balance the needs between support-seeking and self-presentation becomes an important question to investigate. Research shows that supportive communication is a face-threatening act (Goldsmith, 1992). A support-seeker's positive face is threatened when they disclose their stressors and expose their weaknesses to an undifferentiated audience. In addition, revealing negative content in a post potentially violates the norm of positivity bias and further threatens a support-seeker's positive image (Reinecke & Trepte, 2014). Given the complexities presented in supportive communication on SNSs, this project examines how users may overcome these challenges and take advantage of SNSs to elicit effective support.[1]

The first objective of this study is to investigate strategies that support-seekers can use to elicit support on SNSs. Prior research shows that support-seeking posts on SNSs vary in their valence, ranging from negative to positive (Blight, Jagiello, Ruppel, 2015). On one hand, people may want to disclose their stressors to justify their needs for support. On the other hand, they may try to adhere to the norm of positivity bias and project a positive self-image. Guided by the norm of positivity bias, this study examines if support-seeking posts varying in valence would lead to differences in received support. Besides post valence, this study also examines the directness of support request as a potential strategy to seek support. The low social costs associated with lurking on SNSs may make many viewers feel not obligated to respond (Rains & Keating, 2011; Fullwood et al., 2019). A direct request for support may emphasize a support-seeker's need for support and attract an audience's attention to provide support. At least in face-to-face communication, a direct request for support was found to positively affect support provision (MacGeorge, Feng, Burleson, 2011). This strategy is likely to be more important online because many nonverbal cues are filtered out and support needs might be less easily recognized on SNSs. Directly asking for help may then help support-seekers to elicit more support.

In addition to support-seeking strategies, this study also aims to investigate support-seekers' perceptions of received support. Although perceived social support has been studied across channels (Rains & Wright, 2016), very little research has examined perceptions of different forms of social support. SNSs integrate multiple channels and provide users with various means to interact. A support-seeking post, for example, may receive different forms of responses, with textual comments and one-click reactions as the two major forms (Burke & Kraut, 2016). While a textual comment involves substantive content, a one-click reaction provides lightweight reactions. Due to their different nature, these two forms of responses could lead to different perceptions of supportiveness. This study strives to fill the gap by examining whether the perceived supportiveness differs between a comment and a one-click reaction.

5.1 Valence of Support-Seeking Posts, Norm of Positivity Bias, and Self-Presentation

Extant research has examined social support exchange on a variety of

SNSs, including but not limited to, Facebook (Frison & Eggermont, 2020; Youngvorst & High, 2018), Instagram (Wong, Amon, Keep, 2019), and Twitter (Attai et al., 2015; Rui, Chen, Damiano, 2013). These platforms vary in design features and user characteristics (Buccafurri et al., 2015), which may affect supportive communication in different ways. For instance, people tend to engage in more cancer-related support-seeking activities on Twitter than on Instagram (Vraga et al., 2018), perhaps due to the different capacities afforded by Twitter and Instagram, with the former emphasizing texts and the later advocating images.

Despite the differences among popular SNSs, these platforms share some commonalities (Fox & McEvan, 2017; Rains & Brunner, 2015) that entail supportive communication. For example, most SNSs allow users to respond with textual comments and one-click reactions (Carr Wohn, Hayes, 2016), or interact with others in a public or private setting (Youngvorst & High, 2018). In particular, on one hand, high publicness may maximize support-seekers' likelihood to be helped by enabling them to broadcast their feelings, experiences, and thoughts to an entire social network (Carr et al., 2016). On the other hand, the feature of publicness may increase individuals' concerns about self-presentation in support-seeking due to the norm of positivity bias (Reinecke & Trepte, 2014). According to the norm of positivity bias, people in general prefer positive content over negative content. Positive content is perceived as more appropriate than negative content on SNSs (Waterloo et al., 2018). The preference for positive content on SNSs might be attributed in part to emotional contagion (Kramer, Guillory, Hancock, 2014). Kramer, Guillory, and Hancock. (2014) found that Facebook users who viewed fewer negative posts on the platform produced fewer negative posts and more positive posts themselves. The opposite pattern was observed when they viewed fewer positive posts. The findings indicate that positive posts tend to deliver more positive sprits and are thus favored by most SNS users, whereas publicly disclosing stressors and negative feelings may make a discloser appear too emotional or needy (Buehler, 2017).

Considering the impact of positive posts on an audience, posters likely adhere to the norm of positivity bias in online support-seeking and strategically present themselves on public forms of SNSs. Because many support-seeking posts involve negative content, as they reveal stressors and express negative emotions (Blight, Jagiello, Ruppel, 2015), sharing such posts with an undifferentiated audience on SNSs may exacerbate the threat to the poster's positive self-presentation. To mitigate the threats to one's self-presentation, posters may deliberately increase the presence of positive content when seeking-support on channels is high in publicness.

One distinct strategy identified in a thematic study regarding online support is to project optimism in the face of adversity (Buehler, 2017). Along with emotionally distressed experiences, people can also express hope and strength in their support-seeking posts. Another study (Blight, Jagiello, Ruppel, 2015) analyzed users' most recent support-seeking posts on Facebook and concluded that people sought support using positive, negative, or mixed-valence content, with more than half of the posts adopting a positive tone. Overall, strategic framing of a post may positively affect a poster's self-presentation. Instead of showing one's vulnerability and incompetence, a poster displays their strength and grit when faced with obstacles. Viewers therefore may have a more positive impression of the support-seeker and become more motivated to provide support.

The role of popular SNSs such as Facebook, Twitter, and Instagram in supportive communication has been acknowledged in prior research (for a review, see Meng et al., 2017). Support-seekers are found to strategically present positive content in their posts (Buehler, 2017). However, seldom does research examine the effectiveness of this strategy in support solicitation. To address this question, this study examines if support-seeking posts varying in valence differ in number of responses received. Based on online support literature (Blight, Jagiello, Ruppel, 2015; Buehler, 2017), positive posts are defined as posts that only present positive information or deliver positive emotions without mentioning difficulties or bad news; negative posts include posts that only share bad news and difficulties, or deliver negative emotions; and mixed-valence posts contain elements from both positive and negative posts or only disclose neutral content. In addition, this study focuses on two major forms of responses afforded by almost every SNS: textual comments and one-click reactions. Textual comments are composed of messages that involve substantive content whereas one-click reactions are light-weighted alternatives such as "Like" or "Favorite" on SNSs (Burke & Kraut, 2016). According to the norm of positivity bias, positive content tends to elicit favorable impressions and thus may increase people's motivation to help others. Therefore, the following hypothesis is proposed.

H1: The number of comments and one-click reactions received by a support-seeking post will decrease from a positively-valenced post, to a mixed-valenced post, and lastly to a negatively-valenced post.

5.2 Directness of Support-Seeking, Face Threats, and Support Provision

As the first act in supportive communication, support-seeking influences the likelihood and the ways that people provide social support (MacGeorge, Feng, Burleson, 2011). The sensitive interaction systems theory posits that people use both direct and indirect strategies to seek social support (Barbee & Cunningham, 1995). Direct support-seeking strategies include both verbal and nonverbal behaviors that explicitly convey the need for social support. For example, a support-seeker may directly discuss problems with a listener and ask for help, or show obvious distress about their problems through crying. Indirect support-seeking strategies could be subtle and ambiguous. A person may hint at the existence of a problem without directly requesting assistance. Prior research examining offline supportive communication shows that directness of support-seeking affects the chance of being helped (MacGeorge, Feng, Burleson, 2011). Support-seekers who adopt a direct strategy tend to receive more support than those who use an indirect strategy (Barbee & Cunningham, 1995). Compared with an indirect support-seeking strategy, a direct strategy tends to more clearly show people's need for support and motivate others to provide help. Indeed, some people post on SNSs to mainly vent their emotions without a strong desire to seek support. People who do not directly ask for support would perceive more threat presented by others' advice (Goldsmith, 2000). These posters may be inappreciative of support-providers and consider unsolicited support as an intrusion on autonomy (Goldsmith & Fitch, 1997). Due to the concern over others' face needs, many people may refrain providing unsolicited support to distressed people (Goldsmith & Fitch, 1997). A direct support-seeking request, however, unambiguously conveys the desire for support. In addition, direct support-seekers tend to be more receptive to others' support compared to indirect support-seekers (MacGeorge, Feng, Burleson, 2011). Direct support-seeking serves as a green light to give providers permissions to offer help. As a result, people are more willing to provide support, either leaving comments or providing one-click reactions to a direct support-seeker.

To date, directness of support request has been examined in the context of face-to-face supportive communication, with sparse research attention in an online context (Youngvorst & High, 2018). This factor, however, is perhaps more important in the virtual context compared to the offline context. Unlike face-to-face communication where people typically engage in spontaneous communication, posts on SNSs often do not involve simultaneous interaction. The lack of nonverbal and social context cues may make viewers feel less obligated to respond to others' posts (Rains & Keating, 2011). When viewers are aware that a post is shared with a number of others, they may not feel the responsibility to help, Because it is diffused to everyone in the poster's social network and thus viewers become less motivated to offer help (Darley & Latane, 1968; Martin & North, 2015). In addition, overflow of information may make viewers fatigue and easily ignore information posted by others. Sometimes, viewers may even pretend they have not read others' posts, although they already did in fact read them. Therefore, it is imperative to examine how to attract viewers' attention and responses on SNSs. Because extant literature suggests that directness of support request could be an effective way to elicit social support in the offline context (MacGeorge, Feng, Burleson, 2011), the same strategy may also have the potential to enhance viewers' awareness of a poster's support need and increase their motivation to provide help. Therefore, the following hypothesis is proposed.

H2: Compared to support-seekers who indirectly request social support in their posts, those who make direct requests will receive more comments and one-click reactions.

5.3 Forms of Support and Perceived Supportiveness

People use different strategies to obtain social support, but the received feedback may come in different forms and be evaluated differently on their supportiveness. SNSs incoporate multiple channels and provide users with different means to interact with others. Among a wide selection of interaction options, textual comments and one-click reactions function as two major forms of response on SNSs. Textual comments are composed of messages targeting a poster; one-click reactions provide a low-effort alternative with a click of "Like" or other paralinguistic buttons on social media (Burke & Kraut, 2016). One-click reactions are a recent addition to many SNSs to allow users to express their emotions with an easy move. The "Like" button was the first one-click reaction on major SNS Facebook. Now, more reactions, such as "Love" "Sad" and "WOW," have been added to the collection to represent a wide range of emotions. Besides Facebook, other popular SNSs afford users a wide variety of one-click reactions to express their feelings and emotions.

A cross-sectional survey examined the impacts of comments and one-click reactions on Facebook users' psychological well-being (Burke & Kraut, 2016). The results showed that receiving composed communication such as comments had a marginally positive impact on users' well-being, while receiving one-click reactions did not. Likewise, another study regarding social support on Facebook did not find a positive correlation between the number of "likes" and perceived social support (Blight Jagiello, Ruppel, 2015). More investigation into this question revealed that people cared less about the number of one-click reactions but more about who liked their posts. One-click reactions from close others are generally perceived as more supportive than those from distant others (Carr, Wohn, Hayes, 2016). Apart from prior research, which typically examines the relationship between number of comments/one-click reactions and perceived supportiveness, this study tried to investigate if a single comment and a one-click reaction would be perceived differently on their supportiveness.

One-click reactions have been described as light-weight reactions with an absence of language or other substantive content (Hayes, Carr, Wohn, 2016). Because these reactions only take one click to produce, they have become a convenient way to signal viewers' attention and to maintain relationships with minimal effort. Research even shows that leaving a one-click reaction becomes an automatic behavior for many social media users who habitually or repetitively click reactions toward others' posts without much involvement or deliberation (Hayes, Carr, Wohn, 2016). For example, some participants in Hayes and his colleague's study (2016) reported that they sometimes aimlessly liked others' posts for no reasons. Another study revealed that leaving one-click reactions was a low-cost means to maintain social connections, making people feel connected with less close others (Sumner, Ruge-Jones, Alcorn, 2018). Given the ease to produce, a one-click reaction is likely to be perceived as involving little active thought compared to a textual comment. A comment, at least, involves some deliberate thoughts and delivers substantive meanings which require more effort to generate. Therefore, a one-click reaction is likely to be devalued and less appreciated compared with a comment (Sumner, Ruge-Jones, Alcorn, 2018). Due to the different natures and meanings attached to these two forms of response, the following hypothesis is proposed.

H3: People will perceive a textual comment to be more supportive than a one-click reaction on SNSs.

5.4 A Cross-Sectional Survey Testing the Hypotheses

5.4.1 Participants

Upon IRB approval, data were collected from a total of 565 members of Amazon's Mechanical Turk community who resided in the US, spoke English, and self-identified as active users on at least one popular SNS (e.g., Facebook, Twitter). Participants received a payment of three dollars for their participation. A set of filtering criteria was used to clean the data set. Data from 154 participants did not meet specific criteria and were excluded, leaving a total of 411 participants for final analysis. Specifically, a case was deleted if a participant spent less than two minutes ($n = 7$) or more than one hour ($n = 11$) on the survey, or an identified post was not a support-seeking post ($n = 87$), or a post was from a non-SNS platform ($n = 10$), or a participant failed one or more attention checks ($n = 26$), or a participant did not answer questions about comments/one-click reactions ($n = 13$). Of all valid cases, participants were 47.7% female, with a median income of $ 40,000 to $ 49,999 and a median education of 4-year bachelor's degree. The average age was 33.17 ($SD = 8.38$). Participants were 73% White, 7.3% Black or African American, 0.7% American Indian, 8.0% Asian, 0.5% Native Hawaiian, with 6.7%

identifying as "other" and 3.8% identifying as bi-or multi-racial.

5. 4. 2 Procedure

Participants were instructed to log onto a SNS that they frequently visited and to identify the most recent post that they broadcasted to others for emotional support. A support-seeking post is defined as a post that intends to seek comfort, reassurance, validation, or acceptance from others. Each participant was asked to copy and paste their support-seeking post to the survey and to answer questions about their SNS use. The second section asked participants about feedback received on the support-seeking post, including the number of received comments and one-click reactions, content of the first three comments and the first three one-click reactions, perceived supportiveness of the feedback, and other related questions. Participants were last asked about their demographic information and compensated for their participation.

5. 4. 3 Measures

Valence of support-seeking post. All recorded support-seeking posts were coded for their valence to be positive (+ 1), negative (− 1), or mixed (0). A coding manual was developed by the authors based on Blight, Jagiello, Rupple's (2015) and Buehler's (2017) studies. A positive support-seeking post projects optimism, positivity, strength, and hope without mentioning difficulty or distress (e. g. , "Praying everything goes well tonight! Good luck hubby."). A negative post mentions difficulty or distress without a projection of optimism, positivity, strength, and hope (e. g. , "I just lost my job. Someone convince me why I shouldn't feel like an absolute failure."). A mixed-valence post projects optimism, positivity, strength, and hope while mentioning difficulty or distress (e. g. , "It has been a hell of a week. My emotions are everywhere, but I know the good days are ahead."). Two coders completed ten hours' training and independently coded a batch of 94 cases

(22. 87%) for reliability assessment. After reaching satisfactory reliability (Krippendorff's $\alpha = 0.86$), cases were evenly split among the two coders for independent coding. Of all posts, 42.8% ($n = 176$) posts were negatively-valenced, 46. 7% ($n = 192$) posts were of mixed-valence, and 10.5% ($n = 43$) posts were positively-valenced.

Directness of support request. Each post was also dichotomously coded for directness of support request. If a poster directly or explicitly asked for support, the post was coded as direct support seeking ($+1$). If a poster only hinted that support might be needed, the post was coded as indirect support seeking (0). The same two coders coded 94 cases (22.87%) after training and reached good reliability (Krippendorff's $\alpha = 0.86$). Then they each coded half of the cases for directness of support seeking. More than half of the posts ($n = 221$, 53. 8%) involved direct requests and the remaining posts did not ($n = 190$, 46.2%).

Numbers of comments and one-click reactions. Each participant was instructed to report how many comments and one-click reactions that they received on their support-seeking posts. Overall, participants reported that they received 15.31 comments ($SD = 34.83$) and 26.03 one-click reactions ($SD = 57.11$).

Perceived supportiveness of responses. Each participant was also asked about the perceived supportiveness of the first three comments and the first three one-click reactions that they received. A five-item semantic differential scale was used to assess this variable (e. g., "insensitive/sensitive" "unhelpful/helpful" "not encouraging/encouraging").

Control variables. Participants were asked on which SNS platform(s) that they posted the support-seeking message. Because the same message could be posted on several SNS sites, we allowed participants to choose more than one site where the post was shared. Overall, 83.9% of the posts were from Facebook, 11% were from Twitter, and 4. 6% were from Instagram. Other platforms such as Google + only counted for 1.9% of all platforms used for the posts. Participants were also asked about their daily time spent on the identified SNS sites. Due to the importance of relational closeness on perceived support (Carr et al., 2016), this variable was measured with six items on a 5-point Likert-scale (e.g. "How close are you to the commenter?" 1 = *not at all*; 5 = *very much*). Posting time was also included as a control variable because the time lapse may affect people's perceived support.

5.5 Results

The statistical analysis was conducted using R 3.5.0 and its packages "lme4" (v. 1.1-17), "lmerTest" (v. 3.0-1) and "emmeans" (v. 1.3.1). H1 and H2 were tested with multivariate analysis of variance (MANOVA) models, which can take into account the correlation between the two dependent variables (i.e., number of one-click reactions and comments). H3 was tested with a mixed-effect model, which assigns a random effect to each post in order to account for the correlation among the perceived effectiveness among multiple responses received by the same post. Posting time and site of a support-seeking message, average time using the site, sex, age, race, education level, and income were included as control variables in all analyses. In addition, order of a response (i.e., first, second or third), as well as relational closeness between a support-seeker and a respondent was included as control variables in H3.

H1 proposed that the number of comments and one-click reactions received would decrease from positively-valenced posts, to mixed-valenced posts, and last to negatively-valenced posts. To take into account the two dependent variables, the number of comments and one-click reactions using a multivariate analysis of variance (MANOVA) model was jointhy modelled to compare the positively-, negatively-, and mixed-valenced support-seeking posts, while adjusting for the control variables. Based on the MANOVA result, the number of comments and one-click reactions was significantly different among the three post valence groups ($F_{(4,672)} = 3.403$, $p = 0.009$), with both number of comments (F (2,336) = 4.928, $p = 0.008$) and one-click reactions (F (2, 336) = 4.742, $p = 0.009$) being significantly different among the three groups. The number of comments and one-click reactions for each post valence group is listed in Table 5.1. The results showed that negatively-valenced posts received significantly fewer comments ($t = -2.506$, $p = 0.034$) and fewer one-click reactions ($t = -2.548$, $p = 0.030$) than posts with mixed valence. Posts with negative valence also received fewer comments or one-click reactions than the positive valence group, but the differences are not statistically significant for either comments ($t = -1.026$, $p = 0.561$) or one-click reactions ($t = -2.032$, $p = 0.106$). The number of responses received by posts with mixed and positive valence is relatively close for both comments ($t = 0.480$, $p = 0.881$) and one-click reactions ($t = 0.476$, $p = 0.883$). Therefore, H1 was partially supported.

Table 5.1. Number of responses across three conditions of post valence

Valence of support-seeking posts	Number of comments		Number of one-click reaction	
	Mean	SD	Mean	SD
Positive	17.60	23.91	41.25	72.41
Mixed	20.47	47.45	32.29	65.67
Negative	9.16	13.62	16.05	39.63

H2 proposed that support-seekers who made a direct request for support would receive more comments and one-click reactions than those who indirectly sought support. A MANOVA model similar to H1 was used to test this hypothesis. The number of comments and one-click reactions was compared between those who directly requested social support and those who indirectly sought support. The results showed that the number of comments and one-click reactions was significantly different between the two groups (F (2, 336) = 3.725, $p = 0.025$). Specifically, the number of comments was significantly higher for those who directly sought support ($M = 19.77$, $SD =$

45.76) than those who indirectly sought support ($M = 10.39$, $SD = 16.83$), F (1,337) = 7. 460, $p = 0.007$). However, the number of one-click reactions was not significantly different between those who directly requested support ($M = 28.68$, $SD = 65.90$) and those who did not ($M = 23.06$, $SD = 44.89$; F (1,337) = 1.559, $p = 0.213$). H2 was also partially supported.

H3 examined the perceived supportiveness between a comment and a one-click reaction. To test H3, the participants' perceptions of the first three comments and first three one-click reactions were modeled. In order to account for the correlation between the perceptions given by the same subjects, a mixed-effect model which assigns a random intercept for each participant was used. It should be noted that this mixed-effect model is robust to missing data for participants who only reported one or two comments and/or one-click reactions. The perceived supportiveness of a response was regressed on the type of response (i.e., comment or one-click reaction), while adjusting for the order of a response (i.e., first, second, or third), relational closeness, along with the same control variables included in the previous analyses. Partial F-tests are performed on the regression coefficients based on numerator degree of freedom estimated using the Satterthwaite's method. As predicted, the perceived supportiveness for a comment ($M = 5.68$, $SD = 1.28$; $M_{adj} = 5.78$, $SEM = 0.27$) was higher than a one-click reaction ($M = 5.39$, $SD = 1.30$; $M_{adj} = 5.50$, $SEM = 0.27$), F (1, 1537.09) = 43.40, $p < 0.001$. Therefore, H3 was supported. In addition, relational closeness and participant sex were significant predictors for the perceived supportiveness of a response. Specifically, if the relational closeness increased by 1 on the Likert-scale, the perceived supportiveness increased by 0.49, F (1,1793.91) = 385.88, $p < 0.001$. The perceived supportiveness for female participants was 0.26 higher than male participants, F (1, 324.36) = 7.57, $p = 0.006$.

5.6 Discussion

With the objective to help people effectively seek support on SNSs, this study examined two strategies that have the potential to increase people's chance of being helped. Based on an analysis of survey data provided by SNS users, this study found that support-seeking posts containing some positive content were more successful in attracting others' responses than posts only containing negative content. In addition, posts that use a direct support-seeking strategy tend to receive more comments than posts that indirectly ask for help, although the difference on one-click reactions was not significant. Besides support-seeking strategies, this study also examined perceived supportiveness between a comment and a one-click reaction. Overall, a comment was perceived as more supportive compared to a one-click reaction.

This study advanced the online support literature by incorporating the norm of positivity bias into research on support-seeking and provision on SNSs. Consistent with the norm of positivity bias, the results showed that mixed-valenced supporting-seeking posts, which include both positive and negative content, elicited more comments and one-click reactions than negative posts. Contradictory to the prediction, positive posts did not elicit more responses than either mixed-valenced or negative posts. A positive post can project a favorable image of a support-seeker. However, it may not adequately communicate the seeker's support needs because viewers may perceive that the seeker has successfully coped with the stressor (Youngvorst & High, 2018).

Past research has identified the use of a positive tone as a support-seeking strategy on SNSs (Buehler, 2017), yet has not examined communication outcomes of this strategy. Findings in this study validated the effectiveness of this strategy and provided some useful insights into online support seeking. Though disclosing negative information can explicitly communicate people's support needs, merely doing so may lead to an unfavorable impression of a support-seeker and discourage viewers from providing support. Therefore, incorporating some positive content, such as expressing optimism to overcome obstacles, can counterbalance the unfavorable impression delivered by negative content and motivate people to provide more support.

This study also extended the examination of directness of support-seeking from face-to-face communication to the realm of SNSs. The findings revealed different patterns for comments and one-click reactions received on a support-seeking post. As predicted, direct support-seeking helped posters elicit more comments than indirect support-seeking. A direct request for support likely attracts more attention from viewers, who may otherwise ignore one's support need due to a lack of nonverbal cues on SNSs. However, the number of one-click reactions did not differ as a function of directness of support-seeking. Given that one-click reactions engage minimal effort to generate, people may habitually click on these buttons to provide low-effort support, regardless of the directness of support-seeking (Hayes, Carr, Wohn, 2016). While this study focused on verbal forms of support-seeking, future research can advance this line of work by examining a combination of verbal and nonverbal communication in online support exchange, a topic that has received limited research attention (Youngvorst & High, 2018). It would be interesting to examine if nonverbal support-seeking strategies (e. g., posting a distressed picture) would work in a similar or different way as verbal strategies in eliciting support on SNSs.

This study presented the first effort to directly compare the perceived effectiveness of a comment with a one-click reaction in social support. Though both comments and one-click reactions were found to be supportive, the efforts individuals put into the two forms of responses may vary and lead to differences in perceived effectiveness. The results showed that support-seekers perceived comments as more supportive than one-click reactions. Compared with one-click reactions, textual comments require more effort to produce and generally include more substantive meanings that can convey comfort and offer suggestions. In addition, one-click reactions are more homogenous than comments, with many people responding with the exact same one-click reaction (e.g. Love, Like) on a post. Due to the lack of uniqueness, one-click reactions might hardly be noticed by a support-seeker, especially if the seeker received numerous one-click reactions. Because support-seekers appreciate comments more than one-click reactions, those who intend to help others can achieve better outcomes of support by writing up textual comments. One-click reactions, as a low-cost alternative, cannot fully substitute for comments in support provision. Beyond the comparison of comments and one-click reactions on their perceived supportiveness, future research may look into the differences among various types of one-click reactions. For example, Facebook alone provides Like, Love, Haha, Wow, Sad, and Angry buttons, which present different meanings and may be suitable for different situations. Leaving a Haha reaction to a support-seeking post may backfire if a support-seeker is in a sad mood. The effectiveness of one-click reactions may thus differ as a function of post content. It might be acceptable and even encouraging to a positive or mixed-valenced support-seeking post that projects optimism, but inappropriate to like a negative post that only discloses stressors. Comparing the effectiveness of different one-click reactions can provide further guidance on effective support provision on SNSs.

This study has several limitations that present opportunities for future research. First, this study only measured perceived supportiveness of the first three comments and the first three one-click reactions respectively. It is unknown if the difference on perceived supportiveness of comments and one-click reactions would decrease and even diminish when responses accumulate. It is possible that diminishing returns may occur as a poster receives more responses. Alternatively, because one-click reactions provide homogenous responses and are less likely to catch support-seekers' attentions, comments may be perceived as even more supportive than one-click reactions as they accumulate over time. Second, participants may not keep track of the order of one-click reactions that they have received, especially if they have received a lot. Participants may need to click open the one-click reaction buttons to view the order of one-click reactions that they have received and who they have received them from. However, the first a few one-click reactions tend to be better remembered compared with later ones due to the primacy effect. Recalling the first three one-click reactions thus should be a manageable task.

Note

1. A version of this chapter has been published as: Li, Coduto, and Song. (2020). Comments vs. one-click reactions: Seeking and perceiving social support on social network sites. *Journal of Broadcasting & Electronic Media*, 64, 777-793. doi: 10.1080/08838151.2020.1848181.

References

Attai, D.J., Cowher, M.S., Al-Hamadani, M., Schoger, J.M., Staley, A.C., and Landercasper, J. (2015). Twitter social media is an effective tool for breast cancer patient education and support: Patient-reported outcomes by survey. *Journal of Medical Internet Research*, 17(7), 188.

Barbee, A. P., and Cunningham, M. R. (1995). An experimental approach to social support communications: Interactive coping in close relationships. In: B. R. Burleson, ed., *Communication yearbook* 18. Thousand Oaks, CA: Sage, pp. 381-413.

Blight, M. G., Jagiello, K., and Ruppel, E. K. (2015). "Same stuff different day:" A mixed-method study of support seeking on Facebook. *Computers in Human Behavior*, 53 (Supplement C), 366-373. doi: https://doi.org/10.1016/j.chb.2015.07.029.

Buccafurri, F., Lax, G., Nicolazzo, S., and Nocera, A. (2015). Comparing Twitter and Facebook user behavior: Privacy and other aspects. *Computers in Human Behavior*, 52, 87-95.

Buehler, E. M. (2017). "You shouldn't use Facebook for that": Navigating norm violations while seeking emotional support on Facebook. *Social Media + Society*, 3(3), 56-77. doi: 10.1177/205630511 7733225.

Burke, M., and Kraut, R. E. (2016). The relationship between facebook use and well-being depends on communication type and tie strength. *Journal of Computer-Mediated Communication*, 21(4), 265-281. doi: 10. 1111/jcc4.12162.

Carr, C. T., Wohn, D. Y., and Hayes, R. A. (2016). As social support: Relational closeness, automaticity, and interpreting social support from paralinguistic digital affordances in social media. *Computers in Human Behavior*, 62, 385-393. doi: http://dx.doi.org/ 10.1016/j.chb.2016.03.087.

Darley, J. M., and Latane, B. (1968). Bystander intervention in emergencies: Diffusion of responsibility. *Journal of Personality and Social Psychology*, 8 (4), 377-383. https://doi.org/10.1037/h0025589.

Fox, J., and McEwan, B. (2017). Distinguishing technologies for social interaction: The perceived social affordances of communication channels scale. *Communication Monographs*, 84(3), 298-318. doi: 10.1080/ 03637751.2017.1332418.

Frison, E., and Eggermont, S. (2020). Toward an integrated and differential approach to the relationships between loneliness, different types of Facebook use, and adolescents' depressed mood. *Communication Research*, 47(5), 701-728.

Fullwood, C., Chadwick, D., Keep, M., Attrill-Smith, A., Asbury, T., and Kirwan, G. (2019). Lurking towards empowerment: Explaining propensity to engage with online health support groups and its association with positive outcomes. *Computers in Human Behavior*, 90, 131-140. doi: 10.1016/j.chb.2018.08.037.

Goldsmith, D. (1992). Managing conflicting goals in supportive interaction— An integrative theoretical framework. *Communication Research*, 19(2), 264-286. doi: 10.1177/009365092019002007.

Goldsmith, D. J. (2000). Soliciting advice: The role of sequential placement in mitigating face threat. *Communication Monographs*, 67(1), 1-19. doi: 10.1080/03637750009376492.

Goldsmith D. J., and Fitch, K. (1997). The normative context of advice as social support. *Human Communication Research*, 23(4), 454-476. doi: 10.1111/j.1468-2958.1997.tb00406.x.

Hayes, R. A., Carr, C. T., and Wohn, D. Y. (2016). One click, many meanings: Interpreting paralinguistic digital affordances in social media. *Journal of Broadcasting & Electronic Media*, 60(1), 171-187. doi: 10.1080/08838151.2015.1127248.

Kramer, A. D. I., Guillory, J. E., and Hancock, J. T. (2014). Experimental evidence of massive-scale emotional contagion through social networks. *Proceedings of the National Academy of Sciences*, 111(24), 8788-8790. doi: 10.1073/pnas.1320040111.

MacGeorge, E. L., Feng, B., and Burleson, B. R. (2011). Supportive Communication. In: M. L. Knapp, and J. A. Daly, eds., *Handbook of Interpersonal Communication*. Thousand Oaks, CA: Sage, pp. 317-354.

Martin, K. K., and North, A. C. (2015). Diffusion of responsibility on social networking sites. *Computers in Human Behavior*, 44, 124-131. doi: https://doi.org/10.1016/j.chb.2014.11.049.

Meng, J., Martinez, L., Holmstrom, A., Chung, M., and Cox, J. (2017). Research on social networking sites and social support from 2004 to 2015: A narrative review and directions for future research. *Cyberpsychology, Behavior, and Social Networking*, 20, 44-51.

Oh, H. J., and LaRose, R. (2016). Impression management concerns and support-seeking behavior on social network sites. *Computers in Human Behavior*, 57, 38-47.

Rains, S. A., and Brunner, S. R. (2015). What can we learn about social network sites by studying Facebook?: A call and recommendations for research on social network sites. *New Media & Society*, 17, 114-131.

Rains, S. A., and Keating, D. M. (2011). The social dimension of blogging about health: Health blogging, social support, and well-being. *Communication Monographs*, 78(4), 511-534. doi: 10.1080/03637751.2011.618142.

Rains, S. A., and Wright, K. B. (2016). Social support and computer-mediated communication: A state-of-the-art review and agenda for future research. *Annals of the International Communication Association*, 40(1), 175-211. doi: 10.1080/23808985.2015.11735260.

Reinecke, L., and Trepte, S. (2014). Authenticity and well-being on social network sites: A two-wave longitudinal study on the effects of online authenticity and the positivity bias in SNS communication. *Computers in Human Behavior*, 30, 95-102. doi: https://doi.org/10.1016/j.chb.2013.07.030.

Rui, J. R., Chen, Y., and Damiano, A. (2013) Health organizations providing and seeking social support: A Twitter-based content analysis. *Cyberpsycholoy, Behavior, and Social Networking*, 16, 669-673.

Sumner, E. M., Ruge-Jones, L., and Alcorn, D. (2018). A functional approach to the Facebook Like button: An exploration of meaning, interpersonal functionality, and potential alternative response buttons. *New Media & Society*, 20(4), 1451-1469. doi: 10.1177/1461444 817697917.

Vraga, E. K., Stefanidis, A., Lamprianidis, G., Croitoru, A., Crooks, A. T., Delamater, P. L., Pfoser, D., Radzikowski, J. R., and Jacobsen, K. H. (2018). Cancer and social Media: A comparison of traffic about breast cancer, prostate cancer, and other reproductive cancers on Twitter and Instagram. *Journal of Health Communication*, 23(2), 181-189. DOI: 10.1080/10810730.2017.1421730.

Waterloo, S. F., Baumgartner, S. E., Peter, J., and Valkenburg, P. M.

(2018). Norms of online expressions of emotion: Comparing Facebook, Twitter, Instagram, and WhatsApp. *New Media & Society*, 20 (5), 1813-1831. doi: 10.1177/146144481770734.

Wong, D., Amon, K., and Keep, M. (2019). Desire to belong affects Instagram behavior and perceived social support. *Cyberpsychology, Behavior, and Social Networking*, 22, 465-471.

Youngvorst, L. J., and High, A. C. (2018) "Anyone free to chat?": Using technological features to elicit quality support online. *Communication Monographs*, 85, 203-223.

Chapter 6 Willingness to Reply to an Online Support-Seeking Post

While this book primarily focuses on people's actual production of supportive messages to an online support-seeker, the last chapter is devoted to a related but neglected issue of people's willingness to respond to an online support-seeker. Researchers have a growing interest on online support forums and have examined a wide range of aspects, including characteristics of support-seekers (DeAndrea, 2015; Wright, Rains, Banas, 2010), features of support messages (Bunde et al., 2007; Donovan et al., 2014; Feng, Li, Li, 2016), and health outcomes associated with forum usage (Rains & Young, 2009; Wright, 2002). Surprisingly though, considerably less emphasis has been placed on people's willingness to provide support for others on these forums. Little is known about why some people decide to reply to support-seeking posts whereas others stay muted.

Due to high demand for support provision over these forums, a significant number of support-seeking posts have received limited attention or even been ignored. A content analysis on 6000 posts over multiple online communities has revealed that at least a quarter of those posts remained unanswered. With the hope of receiving advice and comfort, a distressed person initiates a support-seeking post. Failure to receive adequate responses not only leaves a support-seeker in a difficult situation with unsolved issues, it may also exacerbate the person's negative feeling of being ignored. Considering the importance of receiving responses on a support-seeking post, the current project investigates factors that contribute to an individual's likelihood to reply to a support-seeking post. In particular, this study looks at how the interaction among a support-seeker and commenters to a support-seeking post would affect subsequent viewers' willingness to reply to the same post.

The other important objective of this study is to examine and extend the spiral of silence (SOS) theory in its application on online support forums. The SOS theory concerns the influence of public opinion on people's willingness to express their own positions (Noelle-Neumann, 1974) and has been applied to different online settings such as social media (Gearhart & Zhang, 2014) and online chat room (Ho & McLeod, 2008; McDevitt, Kiousis, Wahl-Jorgensen, 2003), but not on support forums. In addition, the SOS theory focuses on people's behavioral intention (i. e., willingness to respond) yet pays little attention to communication outcomes (e. g., actual responses). The current study attempts to examine how people would reply to a support-seeking post considering the majority opinion as well as to investigate the association between people's willingness to reply to a support-seeking post and their actual responses. In the sections that follow, literature on online opinion expression and online supportive communication is reviewed. Hypotheses and research questions are proposed and tested with an experiment.

6.1 Spiral of Silence and Benevolent Approach of Online Anonymity

Over the past few decades, the Internet has largely changed the way that people communicate, especially for opinion expression. The emergence of participatory websites such as discussion forums provides an appealing alternative for people to speak out (Walther & Jang, 2012). Unlike FTF communication which requires physical presence of an individual to voice opinions, these participatory websites offer people a shortcut to express opinions by simply posting a message online, without restrictions of time and space (Turner, Grube, Meyers, 2001; White & Dorman, 2001).

More importantly, support forums often provide the option of anonymity to their users. Text-based online communication lacks a variety of nonverbal and context cues which are abundant in FTF communication (Sproull & Kiesler, 1986; Walther & Parks, 2002). Although forum users are often asked to create an online profile prior to their participation, anonymity can still be achieved in a number of ways. For example, most people would use pseudonyms and non-personal pictures in their profiles which bear little resemblance to their offline identities. Even if online users disclose their real names and display real personal pictures, others may lack motivation or ability to verify the truthfulness of such information (Suler, 2004; Yun & Park, 2011). Other information such as gender and age carries even less weight on determining a user's offline identity. To a large extent, people are able to remain anonymous on support forums if they desire so.

Although some scholars have pointed out that a lack of nonverbal cues in computer-mediated communication (CMC) may make communication less personal and even disruptive (Sproull & Kiesler, 1986; Suler, 2004), many others acknowledge the positive effects of anonymity on opinion expression online (Dubrovsky, Kiesler, Sethna, 1991; Rains, 2007). Plentiful evidence has supported the equalization phenomenon in which anonymity on online discussion forums can foster more egalitarian participation among group members (Dubrovsky, Kiesler, Sethna, 1991; Rains, 2005; Siegel et al., 1986). Immersed in an anonymous environment online, people become less aware of status differences and thus feel less pressure from group members, leading to more freedom to voice their own opinions (Siegel et al., 1986). Further, anonymity protects people, especially those who express unpopular opinions, from receiving substantial punishment such as material sanction or physical retaliation (Yun & Park, 2011). People have the opportunity to separate their online identities from their offline ones (Suler, 2004). Whatever they say or act online cannot be directly linked to their lives offline. Although they may still run the risk of being hurt or isolated in online communities, it is much easier for a person to exit or even disappear on a discussion forum without much cost. Put together, anonymous online forum has the potential to become a conductive platform for people with a minority opinion to speak out.

Considering the potential of CMC as a conductive outlet for open discussion, researchers have a growing interest on studying opinion expression in the cyberspace (Gearhart & Zhang, 2014). At the center of this discussion is the question that whether the SOS theory still holds true in the CMC environment (Yun & Park, 2011). The SOS theory postulates that people's willingness to express their views is based on their perceptions of public opinion (Noelle-Neumann, 1974, 1993). Largely driven by fear of social isolation, people constantly monitor their environment and evaluate the climate of opinion. People tend to keep silent if they perceive their opinion is in the minority; whereas people are more likely to speak out when they believe their viewpoint is in the majority (Noelle-Neumann, 1974, 1993).

Research findings to date have been largely mixed with some studies confirming the SOS theory in CMC yet others did not (Gearhart & Zhang, 2014, 2015; Liu & Fahmy, 2011; Yun & Park, 2011). In line with the benevolent approach of anonymity, a body of literature has noted that the spiraling silence phenomenon is attenuated or even disappearing in an online environment (Ho & McLeod, 2008; McDevitt, Kiousis, Wahl-Jorgensen, 2003; Porten-Cheé & Eilders, 2015). Making a comparison of FTF communication and CMC, Ho and McLeod (2008) found that even though participants who were more afraid of being isolated would be less willing to express their opinions, this effect was largely reduced in CMC. To the opposite of spiraling silence, McDevitt, Kiousis, and Wahl-Jorgensen (2003) found in their experiment that people holding a minority opinion on abortion would speak up more actively than those holding a majority opinion in an online chat room. In a similar vein, people who had a discussion on climate change were more likely to express their minority opinion instead of majority opinion in an online setting (Porten-Cheé & Eilders, 2015).

Contradictory to the benevolent approach, however, the other line of research has confirmed the existence of spiraling silence in virtual world (Gearhart & Zhang, 2015; Nekmat & Gonzenbach, 2013). For example, Gearhart and Zhang (2014) found that social networking site users were less likely to speak out when encountering incongruent opinions on political issues from others, yet more willing to express their opinions when encountering congruent opinions. Similarly, an experiment on online discussion over homosexual issue suggested that people who perceived themselves in a minority opinion were less likely to post messages on forums compared to those with a majority opinion (Nekmat & Gonzenbach, 2013). The contradictory perspectives offered by the SOS theory and the benevolent approach of anonymity open up different possibilities for studying people's willingness to speak out online.

6.2. Willingness to Respond and Expressed Opinions on Support Forums

To test the SOS theory, researchers typically use hypothetical scenarios to examine people's willingness to speak out (Yun & Park, 2011). Participants are often presented with a hypothetical discussion on a controversial topic and are asked about their willingness to speak out after learning about others' positions on the topic (Noelle-Neumann, 1993). People's actual responses are not collected even if they are willing to express opinions. Yun and Park (2001) introduced a more ecologically valid method by employing a real forum where people can leave their responses if they are willing to. Although the actual responses were recorded, this study did not report the association between people's willingness to express opinion and the positions in their actual responses. Actual response is equally important, if not more crucial than people's willingness to express opinion. On discussion forums, people not only pay attention to the number of responses posted in a thread, they also heed to the attitudes and positions reflected in the responses. Online support forums, in particular, have high demand on both quantity and quality of responses. Support-seekers initiate a thread on forums with an intention to solicit advice and sympathy. A predicament of receiving no response not only leaves a support-seeker in a helpless and disappointing situation, it may also discourage the person from further utilizing the forum. While receiving no response is frustrating, even worse is the situation of receiving mostly critical responses. A feeling of being opposed by a number of people is more discouraging than having no support. Therefore, a support-seeker not only appreciates receiving responses from others, but also expects high-quality support messages which may offer encouragement, reassurance, and constructive suggestions (MacGeorge, Feng, Burleson, 2011). Therefore, besides examining people's willingness to reply, it is important to look at what people say in their responses to a support-seeking post.

Although the SOS theory does not explicate the association between people's response likelihood and their actual responses, it does provide the ground to make such inferences. According to the SOS theory, people who believe themselves in the majority are more likely to express their opinions than those who perceive themselves in the minority. Therefore, people who are more willing to speak out tend to express opinions in line with the majority opinion.

On support forums, a support-seeking post may elicit a number of responses with different positions. Some messages may show support and sympathy to a support-seeker; whereas others may blame the support-seeker for the distressing situation (Aakhus & Rumsey, 2010; White & Dorman, 2001). Viewers would rely on previous responses to a support-seeking post to gauge the climate of opinion (Li & Feng, 2015). Based on the SOS theory, people who perceive their positions in congruency with previous responses will be more willing to respond to a support-seeking post. Extending this logic, if those people speak out, they tend to express opinions in line with previous responses. Therefore, people who are more willing to respond to a support-seeking post are more likely to express a majority opinion.

The benevolent approach on anonymity, however, may argue the opposite. Extant research has suggested that anonymity in cyberspace, may attenuate, or even reverse the spiraling silence phenomenon (Ho & McLeod, 2008; McDevitt, Kiousis, Wahl-Jorgensen, 2003; Porten-Cheé & Eilders, 2015). Given that users on online support forums are largely anonymous, users who hold a minority opinion towards the support-seeker would face less pressure from others and worry less about being isolated. Extending this logic, people with a minority opinion may be equally, if not be more willing to speak out than those with a majority opinion. Therefore, it is likely that people do not differ in their willingness to speak out no matter what opinions they express in their responses, or people more willing to speak out are more likely to express a minority opinion. Considering the competing rationales based on the SOS theory and the benevolent approach of anonymity, a research question arises.

RQ1: Is a viewer's willingness to respond to a support-seeking post associated with opinion congruency between a viewer's response and previous comments on the post?

6.3 Willingness to Respond and Support-Seeker's Reply

Online supportive communication is an ongoing process that involves turns of give-and-take between parties involved (MacGeorge, Feng, Burleson, 2011). How interactions unfold may affect people's willingness to respond? For example, some researchers found that original posters who ask questions, introduce oneself, and (or) use simpler language were more likely to get responses from others in online communities. On support forums, a support-seeker may reply to previous comments on the original post. Whether and how a support-seeker replies to previous comments may affect subsequent viewers' willingness to respond to the original post.

Extant literature has suggested that receiving some form of feedback would motivate a poster to contribute more to online communities (Cheshire & Antin, 2008; Joyce & Kraut, 2006; Sohn & Leckenby, 2007). Sohn and Lekenby's (2007) experiment revealed that participants who could directly communicate with others would make more voluntary contribution to an online community than those who could not. Joyce and Kraut (2006) found that people who received responses on their posts were more likely to post again online. Cheshire and Antin (2008) demonstrated the positive effect of a feedback mechanism on people's continuous contribution to virtual communities. The studies reviewed above focused on individuals who already contributed, rather than viewers who have not participated. However, it is reasonable to infer that viewers would be motivated to respond to a support-seeking post after reading the support-seeker's reply to others. When viewers witness a support-seeker replying to previous comments, they may expect a high chance of their responses being read and responded by the support-seeker. The anticipation of receiving feedback will thus encourage a viewer to speak out on a support forum. The following hypothesis is proposed.

H1: Viewers are more willing to reply to a support-seeking post which is followed by a support-seeker's reply than to a post without a support seeker's reply.

In addition to presence or absence of a support-seeker's reply, the content in a reply may also exert an influence on viewers' willingness to post. For instance, three feedback types (gratitude, historical reminder, and relative ranking) are effective to encourage repeated contributions in an online community (Cheshire & Antin, 2008). Because the present study only focuses on verbal replies instead of system-generated data (e. g., historical reminder, relative ranking), only gratitude in the three types is examined. Previous research has repeatedly evidenced that gratitude increases a benefactor's prosocial behavior towards the beneficiary or others (Deutsch & Lamberti, 1986; Grant & Gino, 2010; McCullough, et al., 2001). It is thus expected that the positive impact of gratitude would be extended to bystanders such that viewers of an appreciative reply to previous comments would be more motivated to respond to a support-seeking post, compared to viewers of a support-seeker's reply without appreciation.

H2: Viewers exposed to a support-seeker's appreciative reply are more willing to respond to the support-seeking post than those exposed to a support-seeker's inappreciative reply.

6.4 Willingness to Respond and Issue Involvement

Opinion expression is not only affected by others' reactions, it may also be associated with individual differences such as issue involvement. Issue involvement is defined as the extent to which an individual believes that the issue is important/relevant to him/herself (Pfau et al., 2001; Salmon & Neuwirth, 1990). When a person is concerned with an issue, he/she is more likely to speak out regardless of others' positions. Accumulating evidence has suggested that issue involvement was an important predictor of an individual's willingness to express opinion (Gearhart & Zhang, 2014; Moy, Domke, Stamm, 2001; Salmon & Neuwirth, 1990). Some researchers found that people with higher issue involvement were more likely to upload contents on Wikipedia in Korea. Likewise, Gearhart and Zhang (2014) reported that people who perceived more importance on gay bullying were more willing to comment on the topic on social media. On support forums, if viewers consider a discussed issue to be more personally relevant or important, they are expected to be more motivated to speak out.

H3: Issuer involvement is positively associated with a viewer's willingness to reply to a support-seeking post.

6.5 An Experiment Testing the Hypotheses

6.5.1 Participants

260 students from a large state university participated in this study for extra credit. Five participants were excluded because their responses were not successfully saved. The final analysis was based on data from 255 participants (58.8% female), 41.2% male, ranged in age from 18 to 36 years ($M = 21.34$, $SD = 1.84$). The sample included Asian or Pacific Islander ($n = 165$, 64.7%), Caucasian ($n = 48$, 18.8%), Latino ($n = 26$, 10.2%), African American ($n = 8$, 3.1%), Native American ($n = 1$, 0.4%), and others ($n = 7$, 2.7%).

6.5.2 Design

A 2 (others' comments: supportive vs. unsupportive) × 3 (support-seeker's reply to others' comments: no reply vs. appreciative reply vs. inappreciative reply) × 2 (problem topics: roommate conflict vs. internship) factorial design was used in the study. To enhance external validity, this study used the interface of a real forum "forums.student.com". 12 sets of support-seeking posts and others' comments were then embedded in the forum. Participants were able to read, click, and comment on the forum.

Two problem topics were included for the generalizability of findings. One support-seeking post concerned a time conflict problem with a roommate. The support-seeker wanted to study late but the roommate insisted on turning off lights to sleep. The other post described a problem happening in the workplace. The support-seeker was late for work and treated badly by the boss.

To manipulate the supportiveness of others' comments, two sets of eight comments exclusively being supportive or unsupportive were created for each topic. For example, a supportive comment on the internship topic was "Sorry to hear that. You should definitely find a new place to work. If they can't appreciate your talents, someone else will." An unsupportive counterpart was "You are definitely acting entitled. You can't have everything that you want. You just started your internship. Can't you be a little patient?" Comment sets were made comparable in terms of length and reading level.

A support-seeker's reply varied in three conditions: no reply, appreciative reply, or inappreciative reply. Participants assigned to the condition of no reply were not exposed to any responses from the support-seeker. Participants in the condition of appreciative reply would read the following message from the support-seeker: "Thank you so much! I really appreciative all your input!" In the condition of inappreciative reply, the support seeker would say "I want to get more input." A support-seeker's reply would always appear beneath the last comment. Other information (e.g., user profiles) on the forum was kept constant across the 12 versions of web pages.

6.5.3 Procedure

Upon arriving at the lab, participants were greeted by a research assistant and randomly assigned to an experimental condition. Participants were then escorted to a cubicle equipped with a laptop and were informed that they would read a forum post and respond to the original poster. Each participant was asked to create a username before leaving a response. This procedure ensured that participants' responses on the forum could be linked to their survey data. After clicking the button "post a reply," a participant's response would immediately display beneath the last comment (or support-seeker's reply, if applicable). A specific technique was used to make sure that each participant could only view their own responses but not responses from other participants. Once participants submitted responses, the research assistant returned and directed them to the survey system "Qualtrics" where they were asked to complete a questionnaire on their perceptions and opinions regarding the issue and the support-seeker. Participants were then thanked and debriefed.

6. 5. 4 Measures

Willingness to response. Each participant was asked three questions (e.g., "How likely would you respond to the original post if you had the option of not responding?") on a 7-point scale ($1 = no\ chance$, $7 = certain\ to\ happen$) about their likelihood to respond to a support-seeker if they were not instructed to. This scale exhibited high internal consistency ($M = 3.64$, $SD = 1.38$, $\alpha = 0.88$).

Expressed opinion congruency. Participants' responses to a support-seeking post were categorized into three groups (i. e., unsupportive, neutral, and supportive) in terms of the supportiveness towards a support-seeker. In a related project, participants' responses were coded into nine levels on supportiveness which were embedded into the three major groups. To avoid redundant coding, nine levels were collapsed and messages were re-categorized into three groups (levels 1–4 = *unsupportive*, level 5 = *neutral*, levels 6–9 = *supportive*). Two undergraduate coders independently coded 115 overlapping messages based on a nine-level coding hierarchy (Li & Feng, 2015; Krippendorff's $\alpha = 0.75$). The coders resolved the discrepancies through discussions and split the remaining messages to code. After the messages were grouped into three categories, each category was assigned a value ($-1 = unsupportive$, $0 = neutral$, $1 = supportive$). In addition, manipulated comments were assigned the value of either -1 (unsupportive) or 1(supportive). Opinion congruency was then calculated by multiplying the value of a participant' supportiveness by the value of the manipulated comments, resulting in a value of -1, 0, or 1. Opinion congruency increased from -1 to 1. A value of -1 means a participant holds an opposite opinion from others' comments; 0 means a participant is neutral on

167

the issue but still somewhat different from others' position which is either supportive or unsupportive. A value of 1 means a participant expresses an opinion in congruence with others' comments.

Issue relevance. A scale of eight items on a 7-point Likert scale ($1 =$ *strongly disagree*, $7 =$ *strongly agree*) modified from the Personal Involvement Inventory (Zaichkowski, 1985) was used to measure participants' issue relevance. Examples of the items are "The issue means a lot to me" and "The issue is of my concern." The mean of the eight items was computed to create the issue relevance measure ($M = 3.51$, $SD = 1.39$, $\alpha = 0.93$).

Manipulation Check. An eight-item measure on an 11-point scale was constructed to evaluate the supportiveness of the manipulated comment sets (e. g. , "unsupportive-supportive", "negative-positive"). Participants were asked to rate the supportiveness of others' comments as a whole. The mean of the eight items was computed ($M = 6.43$, $SD = 2.67$, $\alpha = 0.91$). Overall, supportive comments ($M = 8.62$, $SD = 1.26$) were perceived to be more supportive than unsupportive comments ($M = 4.20$, $SD = 1.72$), $t(227) = 23.25$, $p < 0.001$. Problem topics had no significant effect on supportiveness of comments.

Appreciativeness in a support-seeker's reply was measured by four bipolar items on an 11-point scale (e. g. , "inappreciative-appreciative"). Across two problem topics, the appreciative reply ($M = 9.55$, $SD = 1.83$) was perceived to be higher on appreciativeness than the inappreciative reply ($M = 6.57$, $SD = 1.86$).

6.6 Results

In order to generalize the results, two problem topics were included in the current study. Preliminary analyses were conducted to examine the possible effects of problem topic on participants' willingness to reply and positions expressed in their message. As expected, the factor of problem topic did not have any significant effects on those variables and was dropped from further analysis.

A one-way ANOVA was run to examine the research question on the association between people's willingness to respond to a support-seeking post and their opinion congruency with previous comments on the post, $F(2, 252) = 2.53$, $p = 0.082$. People who held congruent or incongruent opinions with others' comments did not significantly differ in their willingness to reply.

H1 and H2 together probed the impact of a support-seeker's reply on viewers' willingness to respond to a support-seeking post. A univariate analysis revealed a significant effect for a support-seeker's reply, $F(2, 252) = 10.80$, $p < 0.001$, partial $\eta^2 = 0.08$. A Bonferroni post hoc test indicated that viewers were more likely to reply to a support-seeking post with a support-seeker's reply, either appreciative ($M = 3.73$, $SD = 0.14$) or inappreciative ($M = 4.05$, $SD = 0.14$), compared with the same post without a support-seeker's reply ($M = 3.11$, $SD = 0.16$), $ps < 0.01$. H1 was thus supported. However, viewers' response likelihood did not differ between appreciative and inappreciative reply, $p = 0.37$. H2 was unsupported.

H3 predicted that viewers with higher issue involvement were more willing to respond to a support-seeking post. Consistent with the prediction, viewers' issue involvement is positively associated with their likelihood to respond, $b = .24$, $t = 3.97$, $p < 0.001$. H3 was supported.

6.7 Discussion

Online support forums have provided people a convenient way to exchange social support. However, one challenge facing online support-seekers is the relatively few responses on support-seeking posts. A negligence of someone's support-seeking post may exacerbate an original poster's negative emotions and inhibit his/her coping with stress. The current study took an initiative to examine people's willingness to reply to a support-seeking post online, and its relationship with opinions expressed in their responses. In general, viewers who expressed a majority or minority opinion in their responses to a support-seeker did not differ in their willingness to speak out. Nevertheless, viewers were more likely to respond if a support-seeker interacted with previous commenters and if viewers perceived a post topic to be more personally relevant.

The SOS theory is introduced to this study to examine people's willingness to respond. Previous research examining the SOS theory in a variety of CMC contexts has gained mixed support (Gearhart & Zhang, 2014, 2015; Liu & Fahmy, 2011; Yun & Park, 2011). This study is the first to examine the relevance of the SOS theory to online support forums. Apart from prior studies that focused on people's perception of public opinion and their willingness to speak out, this study extended the SOS theory by looking at the relationship between people's willingness to speak out and opinions expressed in their actual responses. Although the SOS theory does not directly address this question, it has laid the theoretical foundations for such an inference. According to the SOS theory, people holding a majority opinion are more willing to speak out, so their responses will be more consistent with a majority opinion when they are given the chance to express their opinions (Noelle-Neumann, 1974). To the contrast of the spiraling silence, the benevolent approach of anonymity argues that people with an unpopular opinion are equally or more likely to speak out because anonymity safeguards against being isolated (Gearhart & Zhang, 2015; Nekmat & Gonzenbach, 2013). The results were consistent with the latter such that people who expressed a majority or minority opinion in their responses to a support-seeking post did not differ in their response likelihood. The spiral of silence phenomenon is attenuated or even disappearing on online support forums. Anonymity, in a sense, ensures people have more freedom to speak out without overly attending to others' viewpoints. Anonymous channels such as online support forums provide people with a more equalized platform to share their thoughts and opinions. This is beneficial to online support-seekers because it can effectively prevent one-sided opinions. Even though people would like to receive more supportive messages when encounter difficulties, sometimes an opposite position may inspire the support-seeker to approach the problem from a new perspective. In addition, under circumstances that most people are against a support-seeker, someone with a supportive viewpoint might still be willing to speak up for the target.

One caveat to consider is to what extent people's responses indeed reflect their true thoughts, especially for those who are less willing to speak out. The SOS theory postulates that people holding a minority opinion are less willing to speak out due to fear of isolation (Noelle-Neumann, 1974). When those people are requested to speak out, their responses may not mirror their true opinions due to worry of being isolated after voicing unpopular opinions. Instead, they may comply to the majority opinion in their replies to the support-seeker. If this is the case, the majority of replies should be consistent with the majority opinion. This concern was dispelled because only 40.8% of the participants expressed a congruent opinion in their replies to the support-seeker. A new direction for future studies is to gauge the discrepancy between their actual thoughts and expressed opinions, and to determine whether people deliberately conceal their actual thoughts in responses.

An investigation of viewers' responses in relation to their willingness to express opinions extends the SOS theory at a theoretical level. Despite being unsupported on online support forums, this extension of the SOS theory can be tested within other CMC contexts. For example, on social networking sites such as Facebook, users are identifiable and may not be able to take advantage of anonymity to express their unpopular opinions. In fact, a recent study conducted by the Pew Internet Research suggested that Facebook and Twitter users were less willing to discuss the Snowden Leaks on social media if they perceived most others would disagree with them. The tendency of spiraling silence may still exist on those non-anonymous social media platforms. As a result, people who are more willing to speak out tend to express a majority view of point. Future research may test this speculation by examining the spiral of silence and its extension on identifiable CMC platforms.

Further, this study emphasizes the importance of communication by examining viewers' actual responses. Compared with unspoken perceptions, communicative behaviors exert a more immediate impact on a target's attitudes and behaviors. A viewer who silently supports a distressed individual without posting a response does not have a real impact on the support-seeker. In addition, posters who help others are more engaged within the community than lurkers and thus experience more psychological benefits (Batenburg & Das, 2015). More research should be done to examine messages exchanged on support forums.

Besides the general climate of opinion, this study also takes into account the interaction among support-seekers and support-providers in examining viewers' willingness to respond. The results suggested that viewers were more likely to respond to a support-seeking post with the support-seeker's reply compared to the same post without such a reply. This finding indicates that interaction is taken place at an interpersonal level where people may expect reciprocation in communication. A viewer who read a support-seeker's reply to previous comments may expect that the support-seeker will follow the thread and may continue to respond to others' comments. With an anticipation of future interaction with the support-seeker, a viewer might be more motivated to post a reply. This finding provides practical advice for support-seekers who desire more responses from others. In order to get others' attention and receive more responses, a support-seeker should actively engage in interaction with previous commenters, no matter they were being supportive or unsupportive.

Surprisingly though, presence or absence of appreciation in a support-seeker's reply did not make a difference on viewers' willingness to respond. One possible explanation is that the valence of a support-seeker's reply may not be associated with a viewer's response likelihood. For instance, a support-seeker who expresses dissatisfaction to previous comments may motivate more viewers to contribute. It is worth to point out that the manipulation of inappreciative reply in this study may contain a possible confound. Besides expressing no gratitude to previous commenters, the inappreciative reply also involved a direct solicitation of further input, which may potentially motivate viewers to respond to the support-seeker. In this study, people were more willing to respond after viewing the inappreciative reply ($M = 4.05$, $SD = 0.14$) compared with the appreciative reply ($M = 3.73$, $SD = 0.14$), even though the difference was not significant. Future studies should manipulate a support-seeker's reply in a more rigorous way to avoid such confounds. Moreover, gratitude expression is only one of many ways that a support-seeker interacts with commenters. Various forms of a support-seeker's reply, including but not limited to verbal messages, can be explored in future. For example, a support-seeker may endorse a comment by liking or rating the post. It is interesting to compare the effects of nonverbal versus verbal replies on viewers' willingness to speak out.

Several limitations merit some discussion. In order to have a clear pattern of the majority opinion, comments were manipulated to be exclusively supportive or unsupportive, which might be relatively uncommon in reality. To increase external validity of the study, a set of comments could contain both supportive and unsupportive positions with a discernible pattern of the dominant opinion. However, this type of manipulation may impose threat to the internal validity because the order of comments with different valence may have an impact on people's response likelihood (Li, Feng, Bell, 2015). The other limitation pertains to the research procedure. Because this study aimed to compare people's actual responses to their response likelihood, each participant was instructed to leave a reply to the support-seeker. Considering that many forum users are lurkers who do not contribute after reading posts, future research can examine people's likelihood to respond without giving them instructions to do so.

References

Aakhus, M. , and Rumsey, E. (2010). Crafting supportive communication online: A communication design analysis of conflict in an online support group. *Journal of Applied Communication Research*, 38(1), 65-84. doi: 10.1080/00909880903483581.

Batenburg, A. , and Das, E. (2015). Virtual support communities and psychological well-being: The role of optimistic and pessimistic social vomparison strategies. *Journal of Computer-Mediated Communication*, 20(6),585-600. doi: 10.1111/jcc4.12131.

Bunde, M. , Suls, J. , Martin, R. , and Barnett, K. (2007). Online hysterectomy support: Characteristics of website experiences. *Cyberpsychology & Behavior*, 10(1), 80-85. doi: 10.1089/cpb.2006.9989.

Cheshire, C. , and Antin, J. (2008). The social psychological effects of feedback on the production of Internet information pools. *Journal of Computer-Mediated Communication*, 13(3), 705-727. doi: 10.1111/j. 1083-6101.2008.00416.x.

DeAndrea, D. C. (2015). Testing the proclaimed affordances of online support groups in a nationally representative sample of adults seeking mental health assistance. *Journal of Health Commun*, 20(2), 147-156. doi: 10.1080/10810730.2014.914606.

Deutsch, F. M. , and Lamberti, D. M. (1986). Does social approval increase helping? *Personality and Social Psychology Bulletin*, 12(2), 149-157. doi: 10.1177/0146167286122001.

Donovan, E. E. , LeFebvre, L. , Tardif, S. , Brown, L. E. , and Love, B. (2014). Patterns of social support communicated in response to expressions of uncertainty in an online community of young adults with cancer. *Journal of Applied Communication Research*, 42(4), 432-455. doi: 10.1080/00909882.2014.929725.

Dubrovsky, V. J. , Kiesler, S. , and Sethna, B. N. (1991). The equalization phenomenon: Status effects in computer-mediated and face-to-face decision-making groups. *Human-Computer Interaction*, 6(2), 119-146. doi: 10.1207/s15327051hci0602_2.

Eichhorn, K. C. (2008). Soliciting and providing social support over the Internet: An investigation of online eating disorder support groups. *Journal of Computer-Mediated Communication*, 14(1), 67-78. doi: 10.1111/j.1083-6101.2008.01431.x.

Feng, B., and Hyun, M. J. (2012). The influence of friends' instant messenger status on individuals' coping and support-seeking. *Communication Studies*, 63(5), 536-553. doi: 10.1080/10510974.2011.649443.

Feng, B., Li, S., and Li, N. (2006). Is a profile worth a thousand words?: How online support-seeker's profile features may influence the quality of received support messages. *Communication Research*, 43(2), 253-276. doi: 10.1177/0093650213510942.

Gearhart, S., and Zhang, W. (2014). Gay bullying and online opinion expression: Testing spiral of silence in the social media environment. *Social Science Computer Review*, 32(1), 18-36. doi: 10.1177/08944 39313504261.

Gearhart, S., and Zhang, W. (2015). "Was it something I said?" "No, it was something you posted!" A study of the spiral of silence theory in social media contexts. *Cyberpsychol Behav Soc Netw*, 18(4), 208-213. doi: 10.1089/cyber.2014.0443.

Grant, A. M., and Gino, F. (2010). A little thanks goes a long way: Explaining why gratitude expressions motivate prosocial behavior. *Journal of Personality and Social Psychology*, 98(6), 946-955. doi: http://dx.doi.org/10.1037/a0017935.

High, A. C., Oeldorf-Hirsch, A., and Bellur, S. (2014). Misery rarely gets company: The influence of emotional bandwidth on supportive communication on Facebook. *Computers in Human Behavior*, 34, 79-88. doi: http://dx.doi.org/10.1016/j.chb.2014.01.037.

Ho, S. S., and McLeod, D. M. (2008). Social-psychological influences on opinion expression in face-to-face and computer-mediated communication. *Communication Research*, 35(2), 190-207. doi: 10. 1177/009365020 7313159.

Joyce, E., and Kraut, R. E. (2006). Predicting continued participation in newsgroups. *Journal of Computer-Mediated Communication*, 11(3), 723-747. doi: 10.1111/j.1083-6101.2006.00033.x.

Li, S., and Feng, B. (2015). What to say to an online support-seeker?: The influence of others' responses and support-seeker's replies. *Human Communication Research*, 41, 303-326.

Li, S., Feng, B., Chen, M., and Bell, R. A., (2015). Physician review websites: Effects of the proportion and position of negative reviews on readers' willingness to choose the doctor. *Journal of Health Communication*, 20, 453-461.

Liu, X., and Fahmy, S. (2011). Exploring the spiral of silence in the virtual world: Individuals' willingness to express personal opinions in online versus offline settings. *Journal of Media and Communication Studies*(3), 45-57.

MacGeorge, E. L., Feng, B., and Burleson, B. R. (2011). Supportive Communication. In: M. L. Knapp, and J. A. Daly, eds., *Handbook of Interpersonal Communication*. Thousand Oaks, CA: Sage, pp. 317-354.

Maier, C., Laumer, S., Eckhardt, A., and Weitzel, T. (2014). Giving too much social support: Social overload on social networking sites. *European Journal of Information Systems*, 24(5), 447-464.

McDevitt, M., Kiousis, S., and Wahl-Jorgensen, K. (2003). Sprial of moderation: Opinion expression in computer-mediated discussion. *International Journal of Public Opinion Research*, 15(4), 454-470.

McCullough, M. E., Kilpatrick, S. D., Emmons, R. A., and Larson, D. B. (2001). Is gratitude a moral affect? *Psychol Bull*, 127(2), 249-266. doi: http://dx.doi.org/10.1037/0033-2909.127.2.249.

Moy, P., Domke, D., and Stamm, K. (2001). The spiral of silence and public opinion on affirmative action. *Journalism & Mass Communication*

Quarterly, 78, 7-25.

Nekmat, E., and Gonzenbach, W. J. (2013). Multiple opinion climates in online forums: Role of website source reference and within-forum opinion congruency. *Journalism & Mass Communication Quarterly*, 90 (4), 736-756. doi: 10.1177/1077699013503162.

Noelle-Neumann, E. (1974). The spiral of silence: A theory of public opinion. *Journal of Communication*, 24, 43-51.

Noelle-Neumann, E. (1993). *The Spiral of Silence: Public Opinion—Our Social Skin*. 2nd ed. Chicago: University of Chicago Press.

Pfau, M., Szabo, A., Anderson, J., Morrill, J., Zubric, J., and H-Wan, H. H. (2001). The role and impact of affect in the process of resistance to persuasion. *Human Communication Research*, 27(2), 216-252. doi: 10.1111/j.1468-2958.2001.tb00781.x.

Porten-Cheé, P., and Eilders, C. (2015). Spiral of silence online: How online communication affects opinion climate perception and opinion expression regarding the climate change debate. *Studies in Communication Sciences*, 15(1), 143-150. doi: 10.1016/j.scoms.2015.03.002.

Rains, S. A. (2005). Leveling the organizational playing field—Virtually: A meta-analysis of experimental research assessing the impact of group support system use on member influence behaviors. *Communication Research*, 32(2), 193-234. doi: 10.1177/0093650204273763.

Rains, S. A. (2007). The impact of anonymity on perceptions of source credibility and influence in computer-mediated group communication: A test of two competing hypotheses. *Communication Research*, 34 (1), 100-125. doi: 10.1177/00936502062960S4.

Rains, S. A., and Keating, D. M. (2011). The social dimension of blogging about health: Health blogging, social support, and well-being. *Communication Monographs*, 78(4), 511-534. doi: 10.1080/03637751.2011.618142.

Rains, S. A., and Keating, D. M. (2015). Health blogging: An examination of the outcomes associated with making public, written disclosures about health. *Communication Research*, 42(1), 107-133. doi: 10. 1177/ 0093650 212458952.

Rains, S. A., and Young, V. (2009). A meta-analysis of research on formal computer-mediated support groups: Examining group characteristics and health outcomes. *Human Communication Research*, 35(3), 309-336. doi: 10.1111/j.1468-2958.2009.01353.x.

Salmon, C. T., and Neuwirth, K. (1990). Perceptions of opinion "climates" and willingness to discuss the issue of abortion. *Journalism & Mass Communication Quarterly*, 67, 567-577.

Siegel, J., Dubrovsky, V., Kiesler, S., and McGuire, T. W. (1986). Group processes in computer-mediated communication. *Organizational Behavior and Human Decision Processes*, 37(2), 157-187. doi: http://dx.doi. org/10.1016/0749-5978(86)90050-6.

Sohn, D., and Leckenby, J. D. (2007). A structural solution to communication dilemmas in a virtual community. *Journal of Communication*, 57(3), 435-449. doi: 10.1111/j.1460-2466.2007.00351.x.

Sproull, L., and Kiesler, S. (1986). Reducing social context cues: Electronic mail in organizational communication. *Management Science*, 32, 1492-1512.

Suler, J. (2004). The online disinhibition effect. *Cyberpsychol Behav*, 7 (3), 321-326. doi: 10.1089/1094931041291295.

Turner, J. W., Grube, J. A., and Meyers, J. (2001). Developing an optimal match within online communities: An exploration of CMC support communities and traditional support. *Journal of Communication*, 51(2), 231-251. doi: 10.1111/j.1460-2466.2001.tb02879.x.

Turner, J. W., Robinson, J. D., Tian, Y., Neustadtl, A., Angelus, P., Russell, M., and Levine, B. (2013). Can messages make a difference?: The association between E-mail messages and health outcomes in diabetes patients. *Human Communication Research*, 39(2), 252-268. doi: 10.1111/j.1468-2958.2012.01437.x.

Walther, J. B., and Boyd, S. (2002). Attraction to computer-mediated social support. In: C. A. Lin and D. Atkin, eds., *Communication Technology and Society: Audience Adoption and Uses*. Cresskill, NJ: Hampton Press, pp. 153-188.

Walther, J. B., and Jang, J. W. (2012). Communication processes in participatory websites. *Journal of Computer-Mediated Communication*, 18 (1), 2-15. doi: 10.1111/j.1083-6101.2012.01592.x.

Walther, J. B., and Parks, M. R. (2002). Cues filtered out, cues filtered in: Computer-mediated communication and relationships. In: M. L. Knapp and J. A. Daly, eds., *Handbook of Interpersonal Communication*. 3rd ed. Thousand Oaks, CA: Sage, pp. 529-563.

White, M., and Dorman, S. M. (2001). Receiving social support online: Implications for health education. *Health Education Research*, 16(6), 693-707. doi: 10.1093/her/16.6.693.

Wright, K. (2002). Social support within an on-line cancer community: An assessment of emotional support, perceptions of advantages and disadvantages, and motives for using the community from a communication perspective. *Journal of Applied Communication Research*, 30(3), 195-209. doi: 10.1080/00909880216586.

Wright, K. B., Rains, S., and Banas, J. (2010). Weak-tie support network preference and perceived life stress among participants in health-related, computer-mediated support groups. *Journal of Computer-Mediated Communication*, 15(4), 606-624. doi: 10.1111/j.1083-6101.2009.01505.x.

Wright, K. B., and Rains, S. A. (2013). Weak tie support preference and preferred coping styles as predictors of perceived credibility within health-related computer-mediated support groups. *Health Communication*, 1-7. doi: 10.1080/10410236.2012.751084.

Wright, K. B., Rosenberg, J., Egbert, N., Ploeger, N. A., Bernard, D. R., and King, S. (2013). Communication competence, social support, and depression among college students: A model of Facebook and face-to-face support network influence. *Journal of Health Communication*, 18(1),

41-57. doi: 10.1080/10810730.2012.688250.

Yoo, W., Namkoong, K., Choi, M., Shah, D. V., Tsang, S., Hong, Y., and Gustafson, D. H. (2014). Giving and receiving emotional support online: Communication competence as a moderator of psychosocial benefits for women with breast cancer. *Computers in Human Behavior*, 30, 13-22. doi: http://dx.doi.org/10.1016/j.chb.2013.07.024.

Yun, G. W., and Park, S.-Y. (2011). Selective posting: Willingness to post a message online. *Journal of Computer-Mediated Communication*, 16 (2), 201-227. doi: 10.1111/j.1083-6101.2010.01533.x.

Zaichkowsky, J. L. (1985). Measuring the involvement construct. *Journal of Consumer Research*, 12, 341-352.

图书在版编目（CIP）数据

数字时代的社会支持研究 = Communicating Social
Support in the Digital Age：英文 / 李思悦著. —
杭州：浙江大学出版社，2022.3
ISBN 978-7-308-22359-1

Ⅰ.①数… Ⅱ.①李… Ⅲ.①传播媒介—研究—英文
Ⅳ.①G206.2

中国版本图书馆 CIP 数据核字(2022)第 032136 号

Communicating Social Support in the Digital Age
数字时代的社会支持研究

李思悦　著

策划编辑	吴伟伟
责任编辑	宁　檬　马一萍
责任校对	李瑞雪
封面设计	雷建军
出版发行	浙江大学出版社
	（杭州市天目山路 148 号　邮政编码 310007）
	（网址：http://www.zjupress.com）
排　　版	杭州青翊图文设计有限公司
印　　刷	广东虎彩云印刷有限公司绍兴分公司
开　　本	710mm×1000mm　1/16
印　　张	11.75
字　　数	274 千
版 印 次	2022 年 3 月第 1 版　2022 年 3 月第 1 次印刷
书　　号	ISBN 978-7-308-22359-1
定　　价	48.00 元

浙江大学出版社市场运营中心联系方式：0571－88925591；http://zjdxcbs.tmall.com